French Investment in Colonial Cameroon

Society and Politics in Africa

Yakubu Saaka
General Editor

Vol. 20

PETER LANG
New York • Washington, D.C./Baltimore • Bern
Frankfurt am Main • Berlin • Brussels • Vienna • Oxford

Martin Atangana

French Investment in Colonial Cameroon

The FIDES Era (1946–1957)

PETER LANG
New York • Washington, D.C./Baltimore • Bern
Frankfurt am Main • Berlin • Brussels • Vienna • Oxford

Library of Congress Cataloging-in-Publication Data

Atangana, Martin-René.
French investment in colonial Cameroon: the FIDES era (1946–1957) /
Martin Atangana.
p. cm. — (Society and politics in Africa; v. 20)
Includes bibliographical references and index.
1. Investments, French—Cameroon—History—20th century. I. Title.
HG5869.A3A83 332.67'3440671109045—dc22 2008046410
ISBN 978-1-4331-0464-0
ISSN 1083-3323

Bibliographic information published by **Die Deutsche Bibliothek**.
Die Deutsche Bibliothek lists this publication in the "Deutsche
Nationalbibliografie"; detailed bibliographic data is available
on the Internet at http://dnb.ddb.de/.

29 Broadway, 18th floor, New York, NY 10006
www.peterlang.com

Printed in the United States of America

Contents

Tables

Figures

Acronyms

AEF	Afrique Equatoriale Française
AICDG	Archives de l'Institut Charles de Gaulle, Paris.
ALUCAM	Société Aluminium du Cameroun.
ANCAM	Archives Nationales du Cameroun, Yaoundé
ANSOM	Archives Nationales, Section d'Outre Mer, Aix-en-Provence
ANU	Archives des Nations Unies, New York
ARCAM	Assemblée Représentative du Cameroun
ATCAM	Assemblée Territoriale du Cameroun
CCFOM	Caisse Centrale de la France d'Outre Mer
CFA	Colonies Françaises d'Afrique or Communauté Financière Africaine
CREDICAM	Crédit du Cameroun
ENELCAM	Energie Electrique du Cameroun
ENFOM	Ecole Nationale de la France d'Outre Mer
FDSE	Faculté de Droit et des Sciences Economiques
FEA	French Equatorial Africa
FIDES	Fonds d'Investissement pour le Développement Economique et Social
FWA	French West Africa
IEDES	Institut d'Etude du Développement Economique et Social
JOC	Journal Officiel du Cameroun
JOCF	Journal Officiel du Cameroun Français
JORF	Journal Officiel de la République Française
ORSTOM	Office de la Recherche Scientifique et Technique d'Outre Mer
SIC	Société Immobilière du Cameroun
SIP	Société Indigène de Prévoyance
SEREPCA	Société d'Exploitation et de Recherches Pétrolières du Cameroun
UN	United Nations
UPC	Union des Populations du Cameroun

5.

6.

Preface

This book is the translation of part of my work *Capitalisme et nationalisme au Cameroun au lendemain de la Seconde Guerre mondiale* (Paris, Publications de la Sorbonne, 1998). Whereas my French book explored the political, economic, and social forces involved in the Franco-Cameroonian relationship, the English edition deals exclusively with the financial and economic factors of these relations during the decade that followed the Second World War. It offers an analysis of the program for the development of French overseas colonies known as *Fonds d'Investissement pour le Developpement Economique et Social des territoires d'outre mer* (FIDES) and its socio-economic impact in Cameroon. I have reorganized the original chapters into more detailed chapters and incorporated figures to better support and illustrate my arguments.

The decision to translate my work was made with the hope that it will expand the existing limited literature in English on the history of Cameroon, and make my work available to English-speaking scholars, students, and general readers.

This work would not have been possible without the generous support of various people and institutions. I would first like to thank Bea Vidacs who translated my work from French to English. The translation was funded through a 2001-2002 PSC-CUNY Research Award that I was granted by the Research Foundation of the City University of New York. I gratefully acknowledge that financial support. I also wish to thank the staffs of the following libraries where I conducted my research: *Bibliothèque de Documentation Internationale Contemporaine* (BDIC, Nanterre); *Documentation Française* (Paris); *Bibliothèque Nationale* (Paris); *Bibliothèque Nationale Annexe* (Versailles); *Institut National de la Statistique et des Etudes Economiques* (INSEE, Paris); the Dag Hammarskjold Library (New York); *Archives Nationales, section d'outre mer* (Aix-en-Provence); *Archives Nationales* (Yaoundé); and *Institut Charles de Gaulle* (Paris).

I am very grateful to Evelyn Ackerman (Lehman College and The Graduate Center of The City University of New York) who read my manuscript in its entirety and made corrections and invaluable comments. I also feel indebted to the following individuals, for sharing their wealth of information with me, as well as their advice and critiques: René Girault (University of Paris 1 Panthéon-Sorbonne); Jean Fremigacci (*Centre de Recherches Africaines*, Paris); François Dikoumé, Adalbert Owona, and Léon Kaptue (University of Yaoundé); Dieudonné Oyono (*Institut des Relations Internationales du Cameroun*); René Gobé (*Chambre d'Agriculture de Yaoundé*); and Howard Ruttenberg (York College of the City University of New York). I must also mention Kizzy Charles, Elizabeth Howitt, and Vanessa Grande who helped with the editing and formatting of my manuscript and figures.

Finally, my thanks go to my wife Lois Atangana and her family in New York, my son Charles Atangana, and my family in Cameroon, for their enduring love and support.

Introduction

At the end of the Second World War France and her colonies found themselves in a weakened state, and their infrastructure was partly destroyed or in a state of disuse. The establishment of an economic plan seemed to be a necessity to mend the national and imperial economy. Parallel to the *Plan Monnet* which was the first plan adopted in France for the development of the national economy, the law of April 30, 1946, voted by the French National Assembly established a long term program for the development of France's overseas territories entitled *Fonds d'Investissement pour le Développement Economique et Social des Territoires d'Outre Mer* (FIDES).

This book is an analysis of French investments in Cameroon during the FIDES years (1946–1956). In the 1950s the French colonial empire appeared to be one of the principal bastions of French power. Cameroon was one of the areas of French Black Africa in which France had a great interest after 1945. France invested in Cameroon alone almost as much as she did in French Equatorial Africa, a federation which was much larger and more populous. But since colonial officials, civil servants, and researchers have always grouped Cameroon together with the territories of French Equatorial Africa which were seen as less important, it did not receive the attention it deserved from economists and economic historians. Franco-Cameroonian financial relations and the question of French investments and their impact in Cameroon in the post-war decade are among the problems that have been neglected. The goal of this study is to help fill this gap and make a contribution to this aspect of the history of Cameroon.

The analysis of the financial relationship between Cameroon and France after the Second World War offered in this study is not simply a matter of creating a balance sheet. Numbers are certainly necessary. However, they do not provide any kind of certainty and objectivity. Neither will it be a question of measuring how much Cameroon had cost and contributed to France. This would be a useless exercise which mostly fits, in the case of the French colonial empire in general, into the ideological combats decolonization gave rise to. For those who asked themselves this question in the 1950s and who are still asking it these days, it either leads to the condemnation of French colonialism by calling attention to the benefits France derived from it or serves to absolve the *métropole* because of its generosity. Finally it does not simply try to evaluate the place of Cameroon among the other territories under French rule, given that the conditions varied from one territory to another.

What has to be appreciated is the role played by Cameroon in the dynamics of French capitalism and the part played by this capitalism in the development of the territory. Consequently, I shall assess the movements of capital between Cameroon and France and especially the export of French capital to Cameroon, and the impact of French investment in Cameroon from 1946 to 1956.

Assessing French investment in colonial Cameroon during the FIDES era is not an easy task. What should one understand by "French investment in colonial Cameroon"? What should be measured? What reality should be captured? Several factors need to be taken into consideration in this assessment.

First of all the power that direct political domination granted to France allowed her to channel Cameroon's resources and expenditure according to the need of the *métropole*, and to finance a significant part of the basic infrastructure by using the territory's budget. An examination of the investment made in Cameroon in relation to the local budget will permit a measurement of the amount of metropolitan capital exported to Cameroon. Capital exports quantify French economic intervention in Cameroon and measure the ability of the colonial state to impose its views and authority.

But an assessment of French investment from the point of view of capital exportation alone is not sufficient. It is also necessary to take into consideration investments directed by France to the *mise en valeur* (development) of Cameroon, that is to say, to capital accumulation. The elements involved here include investment made in Cameroon with the local budget, the French budget, FIDES and CCFOM funds, and the reinvestment of profits. In addition, the military and civil operating expenses paid by the French Government for Cameroon should also be considered.

A measurement of financial flows between France and Cameroon allows an evaluation of the arbitrage between financial organizations and industrial firms faced with various investment opportunities in Cameroon. Measuring the totality of investments in Cameroon can help evaluate the power that the colonial assets gave to the *métropole*, and especially to determine the consequences of investments on the internal structures of the Cameroonian economy and society. These are two distinct and complementary analytical approaches which offer the possibility to "measure" and "evaluate," and answer some fundamental questions: what was the financial burden of Cameroon on France? What was the importance of Cameroon to the *métropole*? Did France's public intervention serve to direct the exploitation of the territory in the interest of France or did it serve to promote the interests of Cameroon? The answers to these questions will be found in this book.

It is hard to define French investment in Cameroon, because it has a long history which is hidden and obscured. The history of Cameroon is intertwined with that of three colonial powers: Germany, France and Great Britain, as well as the Mandate System of the League of Nations, and the Trusteeship System of the United Nations. Therefore, documents pertaining to this history are spread over three continents. The scattered nature and even the lack of documentation contribute to render the history of French investment in Cameroon confusing, obscuring and unintelligible.

The absence of economic monographs further complicates the study of French investment in Cameroon, and especially of its actual influence on the economic development of the territory. However, this lack of national-level economic monographs would not be an insurmountable difficulty if the balance of payments for Cameroon covering a sufficiently long time period were available, and especially for the period under consideration here (1946–1956). The balance of everyday operations (essentially "capital revenue") and of capital would have made it possible to follow the evolution of French investment. Unfortunately, this approach is not possible for various reasons.

The theory of assimilation which incorporated the African countries under French rule within the geopolitical field of France (in the franc zone) during the colonial era and even for several years during the post-colonial era led to the establishment of a unitary balance of payments between the entirety of the franc zone and the outside world. Up to a certain period there was no balance of payments between France and the rest of the franc zone. The first balance of payments of this kind was established in 1968. Until that date, and despite the activities of the Monetary Committee of the franc zone, medium and long term movements of capital (especially of private capital) only appeared in the adjustments column or "invisible operations" which the Monetary Committee of the franc zone labeled "unidentified operations." It was not until the year 1968 that decrees relating to the adoption of a model of balance of payments to be applied systematically started to be published in Africa. Thus, there is no balance of payment between France and Cameroon prior to 1968. In order to carry out research for this work it was necessary to resort to other sources including archival documents and statistical works.

Taking into consideration the above factors this book was organized in nine chapters. In the opening chapter, the major developments that led to the birth of the FIDES program will be explored. The second chapter will explain the organization of FIDES and the early stages of this program in Cameroon. The third and fourth chapters will look at the implementation of the two FIDES

Four-Year Plans. The financial assessment of public investment in Cameroon during the FIDES era will be made in chapter five, while chapter six and seven will discuss the development of private investment during the same period. Finally, in the two last chapters the effects of French investments on the budget of colonial Cameroon and on the territory's social and economic structures will be analyzed.

Chapter 1

The Emergence of FIDES

The Political Framework: The Post-War New Order

Two factors were of fundamental significance regarding the relationship between Cameroon and France after the Second World War: the constitutional changes concerning French Africa in the Constitution of the Fourth Republic, and the placing of Cameroon and Togo under the Trusteeship System of the United Nations.

The Constitution of October 1946

The constitution which created the Fourth Republic in France was approved by referendum on October 13, 1946, and took effect on December 24, 1946. It emphasized the doctrine of assimilation and transformed the federalist hopes of the Brazzaville Conference into a centralized French Union[1] comprising metropolitan France, the overseas departments and territories, and the associated states and territories. Cameroon and Togo were incorporated into the French Union as "associated territories." Also, the new constitution gave the inhabitants of the French territories of Africa the right to elect representatives to the parliamentary bodies in Paris. Cameroon was represented first by three and then by four deputies in the National Assembly, three members on the *Conseil de la République* (Senate), and five representatives in the Assembly of the French Union.

The most important political reform of 1946 was certainly the creation of local representative assemblies in the territories under French rule.[2] In Cameroon, the *Assemblée Représentative Camerounaise* (ARCAM) was created by decree on October 25, 1946. The law of January 6, 1952, changed ARCAM to *Assemblée Territoriale du Cameroon* (ATCAM) and modified its composition. The number of representatives rose from 16 to 18 for– the first college (that of the French) and from 24 to 32 for the second college (that of Cameroonians).

To understand this double college system, it should be explained that like all the inhabitants of France's dependent territories, Cameroonians were made citizens of the French Union by the Constitution of 1946. However, this constitution distinguished between citizens with civil law status (French citizens and Cameroonians who had acquired civil law status) and citizens with personal status, that is to say, the great majority of the indigenous population. The first category had the right to vote and constituted the first electoral college. In the second category only those who satisfied a certain number of specific conditions had the right to vote and constituted the second college.[3] In the case of ARCAM, for example, the 2,611 voters registered in the first college elected sixteen representatives, while the 38,976 registered in the second college elected eighteen, and the High Commissioner of France in Cameroon appointed six other Africans to the assembly. The disparity in these numbers becomes even clearer if we mention that the 4,000 French citizens with civil status had sixteen elected officials and the twenty-four others represented three million Cameroonians. ATCAM, the assembly of 1952, was enlarged to include 50 members of which 18 represented some 12,000 French people in Cameroon and 32 represented 3 million Cameroonians.

The sphere of authority of the assembly of Cameroon extended to several aspects of the life of the territory. In the financial field, for example, the Assembly deliberated and voted on the budget. It had spending initiative. The financial autonomy of Cameroon seemed quite strong since the territory retained the totality of its revenue. The International Trusteeship System influenced the fiscal system and the international import-export trade; it was the open door policy which had been instituted in 1884 at the Berlin Conference for the Congo Basin. Under it, Cameroon could establish a wide variety of taxes and duties, including the right of importation and exportation. The powers of the Cameroonian Assembly also extended to the patrimony and above all to the economic and social domains. Thus, this Assembly deliberated on the programs of economic and social development planning in collaboration with the Board of Directors of FIDES. Likewise it deliberated on the problem of incentives for production, the organization of savings banks and all that concerned co-operatives. However, the extent of the powers of the Cameroonian Assembly should not be overstated. This assembly was essentially advisory in nature and its powers were vague.

It is clear that the political changes just analyzed provided the European community of Cameroon with a solid institutional base which enabled it to prevent political reforms. "In fact, the political institutions in Cameroon—and representation in the metropolitan assemblies—were effectively monopolized by three forces: the French colonial administration, the white settler society, and Cameroonians who did not threaten the first two. The predominance of these three collaborating forces was maintained through the wide use of the two-college system which granted political representation to the Europeans greatly disproportionate to their numbers; and secondly, by the very restrictive franchise determining which Cameroonians were allowed to vote."[4]

The double college was the most important objection that could be raised against the assembly of Cameroon and a great source of discontent for Cameroonians. The explanation provided on this matter by the colonial administration to the UN Visiting Mission in 1952 was very clear. It fitted with the government's line:

> At Cameroon's current developmental level the system of double college is still necessary to preserve the interests of the Europeans of the territory, whose contribution is indispensable for its economic development.[5]

The officials charged with administering the territory made the further observation to the UN Mission:

> At present the elected members of the first college can enlighten their colleagues regarding certain economic problems, in particular on the question of the necessity of not taking certain steps likely to alarm or discourage French or foreign external private investments.... [6]

As for the *colons* (settlers) of Cameroon, they believed that with the institution of the single electoral college "the Europeans will be definitively put aside, without it being taken into consideration that 9/10 (if not more) of the economic activity of the overseas territories, almost all of the private capital invested, mining, industrialization, the important businesses of transportation and transit, banking, trade with the *métropole* and with foreign countries etc, are done by the European element.[7]

Various actions were taken by the representatives of Cameroon in the parliamentary bodies in Paris to have the double college abolished. These representatives included Douala Manga Bell, deputy of Cameroon at the National Assembly; Ahmadou Ahidjo, André-Marie Mbida, and Paul Soppo Priso, representatives of Cameroon at the Assembly of the French Union.[8] In the territory, several forces expressed their disagreement: the *Kumzse*, traditional association of the Bamiléké people, demanded the single college;[9] the United Nations Mission of 1949 reported that the *Ngondo*, traditional association of the Duala people, protested against the institution of the double college.[10] The Mission of 1952 pointed out that "the maintenance of the double college has aroused lively criticism among the *évolués* [assimilated] of Cameroon (especially among such political parties as the Cameroonian section of the Socialist Party, *Evolution Sociale Camerounaise* and the *Union des*

Populations du Cameroun (UPC)."[11] The criticisms were generally based on two main factors. On the one hand, the system of the double electoral college constituted racial discrimination; on the other, if the system of a single electoral college had been instituted in French Togo, it should equally be instituted in Cameroon which had the same status. Based on the information it obtained, the UN Mission of 1952 considered that "it would be desirable to institute the single electoral college system as soon as possible in Cameroon." The French succeeded in maintaining this system up until the *Loi Cadre* (Outline Law) of 1956. Indeed it was Article 10 of this law that introduced universal suffrage for all political and administrative elections.[12]

The Trusteeship Agreement

Initially, the French Government did not accept to place Cameroon and Togo under the new Trusteeship system established at the San Francisco Conference of April 1945, just as it had at first refused the Mandate status for the two territories at the end of the First World War. But as in the earlier case, it soon relented under pressure from other governments, among which were the United States and Great Britain.[13] The French opposition completely disappeared when Bevin, the British Foreign Secretary, announced on January 17, 1946, that the former British mandates of Tanganyika, British Cameroon and Togo would be placed under the International Trusteeship System.

A text was proposed by the French and eventually adopted by the General Assembly of the United Nations on December 13, 1946. An analysis of this text shows that France agreed: to respect the primacy of the interests of the population of Cameroon and to develop their gradual participation in the administration of their territory; to assure and safeguard their security; to defend their economic interests and property rights; to maintain the open door policy and to ensure the equal treatment of all members of the United Nations in economic matters; to ensure the intellectual progress of the Cameroonians by developing primary, secondary and vocational education; to facilitate freedom of conscience and worship and to aid the work of missionaries of every nationality and their educational, medical and social activities; to assure freedom of expression and association in Cameroon; and to allow the oversight of the Trusteeship Council.

In return France could: administer Cameroon as an integral part of its own territory; establish if necessary—but after consultation with the local assembly—customs, fiscal or administrative unions with other territories; establish military bases or maintain troops in the territory with the goal of maintaining peace and international security; set up public commercial or industrial monopolies deemed beneficial to the populations; demand reciprocal treatment in economic matters for the territory from countries that benefit from the open door system; organize popular elections to allow the populations to express themselves on the subject of their political system.[14]

The terms of the Trusteeship Agreement caused a lot of discontent among a variety of forces in Cameroonian society. The UN Visiting Mission of 1949 reported that it had "received requests suggesting the revision of the Trusteeship Agreement, notably with regard to the clause of the agreement according to which the territory would be administered as an integral part of the French territory."[15] This particular clause which was included in Article Four was the main focus of Cameroonian criticisms of the Trusteeship Agreement. The dissatisfaction also stemmed from the fact that the proposed agreement had not been submitted for the approval of the indigenous population before being presented to the United Nations.

The power that guaranteed France direct political domination allowed her to formulate an economic and financial policy orientation in the empire based on the needs of the metropolitan country. This is what clearly appears in another important post-war reform: the *FIDES* plan.

The Origins and Birth of FIDES

At the end of the Second World War, France and her colonies had been drained to their limit, their infrastructure partially destroyed or completely worn out. The adoption of a plan seemed to be necessary for the re-launching of the national and imperial economy. The first economic plan adopted by the French for the development of the national economy was the *Plan Monnet.*[16] Paralleling this plan, the law of April 30, 1946, laid down the principles of an economic and social development program for the overseas territories. This program came to be known as *Fonds d'Investissement pour le Développement Economique et Social des Territoires d'Outre Mer* (FIDES). It was also sometimes referred to as *le Plan* (the Plan). To discuss this plan, it is necessary to first recall its origins which can be found in the Sarraut Project of 1921, the Colonial Conference of 1935, and the Brazzaville Conference of 1944.

The Sarraut Project (1921)

It can be said that the Plan originated in the Sarraut Project of 1921.

> The time has come to substitute an overall and precise plan of action for the isolated and vague guidelines. This is all the more possible since today the period of territorial growth is over for our overseas domain. Relieved henceforth of the obligations of conquest, the effort of the French can now be devoted entirely to the organization of the

> full exploitation of their patrimony. The sovereign interest of France in rebuilding the economy, after a war in which its heroism saved the fate of its colonies, coincides today with the interests of every colonial possession to confidently design the general plans creating a united vision for the organization of the overall guidelines for the task of development. This united vision should organize the multiple tasks of all these workers under one overarching rule and should, through the single unceasing will of the nation, overcome the uncertainties and the upsets which had characterized the now past process of its exploitation in our overseas territories.
> This is the precise goal of the present project.[17]

This is how Albert Sarraut, the French Minister of Colonies, spoke during a parliamentary session on April 12, 1921, in a 90-page preamble in the *Journal Officiel* (JORF) to define the goal of his bill aimed at establishing a program to develop the French colonies. This document not only revealed the principles and methods of a new colonial policy but also gave an overview of the economic value of the French colonial domain and its contribution not only to the French war effort, but also to its recovery. The proposed bill to which this voluminous preamble was attached as an appendix gave a detailed list in its first article of the public works programs to be carried out in the overseas territories. The Sarraut project dedicated twenty pages to Cameroon and provided maps of the port of Douala, one of which is very detailed. The project focused primarily on the ports and the communication network.

Unfortunately, the Sarraut project failed. Some observers have attributed this failure to the absence in the plan of concrete measures about the financial means necessary for its execution.[18] This view is clearly expressed by Armand Jean-François:

> The government was perhaps not well-inspired when it failed to incorporate any articles in the project itself about the financial means which would have ensured its execution. Certainly there was enthusiasm about the Minister's plan. But certain events occurred which took precedence in public opinion. At the time France was in the throes of such financial difficulties that she deemed it her duty to try to remove the considerable internal obstacles which the development of the colonies seemed to demand. The enthusiasm of the first days diminished and with it the interest in colonial affairs.[19]

Thus, no attention whatsoever was paid, as indicated by Jean-François, either to the requests for modification of the project made by Deputy Rocques and several of his colleagues in 1921, or to the bill proposed by Senators Messimy and Monzy in 1925, which demanded the granting of incentives to the new industrial or agricultural companies in the colonies, or, finally, to the proposal of Daladier, which demanded the carrying out of a general development program of production and trade in the colonies. Edouard Bonnefous also evoked financial reasons to explain the failure of the Sarraut project when he wrote that

> To finance railways, ports, the regulation of rivers, sanitation works, and so many other urgent projects, they envisioned then an expenditure of 4 billion (old) francs to be spread over ten to twelve years, that is to say about 130 billion francs of 1950. Only with the support of a State organization could such a project succeed. The Minister proposed the creation of *Crédit National des Colonies* [National Bank of the Colonies]....
> The financial market, from which numerous other reconstruction loans were expected, was not up to the task of meeting the obligations which might have been issued by this *Crédit National des Colonies*. The project was abandoned.[20]

But financial factors alone are not sufficient to explain the failure of the Sarraut Project. The lack of support it encountered is also due to other reasons especially the doctrine of the colonial pact (*pacte colonial*) proclaimed by French industrialists according to which the colonies should remain the reservoirs of raw materials and outlets for French manufactured products.

The Colonial Conference (1934–1935)

The Colonial Conference of 1934–1935 had the clear intention of challenging the dogma of the colonial pact by making the point that "economic development in the colonies is necessary for the intensification of trade." During this conference the *Comité des Industries de l'Empire* (Committee for the Industries of the Empire) stated:

> There is no question that the development of the new regions of whose fate a great country takes charge cannot be fully realized unless they are gradually turned into complex economies and evolve from a rudimentary stage of development to a more developed or better organized one of mostly diversified activities.[21]

The Colonial Conference made very specific proposals aimed at directly or indirectly protecting colonial producers. First there were indirect protectionist measures taken against foreign competition. The first of these consisted of raising customs rates in France for those imported products that were similar to colonial products, including banana, citrus fruits, oleaginous plants, lead, zinc, coffee, tea, and other products. In return, such French products as salt and tobacco were protected against foreign competition by raising colonial customs rates. Moreover, certain direct protectionist measures were also envisioned such as: incentives to producers of certain much needed products including banana, coffee, pineapple, manioc, rubber, tobacco, sisal, cotton, and flax; the lowering of customs duty; the granting of the duty free entry of a quota of goods to France; tax relief to forestry development, rubber plantations and to oleaginous crop production; the lifting of all taxes on indispensable equipment for the modernization or creation of factories necessary for the development of the colonies (sawmills, manufacture of fuel, decortication of peanuts, etc).

Financial measures were also envisioned: the granting of land for the creation of new industries; the granting of medium term credit by the *Crédit Colonial* to private firms which modernized their technical equipment; the exemption from French taxes for colonial companies during at least the first years of their colonial activities to facilitate the creation of new colonial companies and to thus help the development of the colony; the establishment of the official headquarters of these new companies in France to ensure that only French fiscal legislation applied to them; the granting of short term credit to agricultural producers.

All of this pre-supposed a modification in the economic policies of the colonial administration. Consequently, a certain number of measures were suggested, such as: the obligation of colonial administrations to use colonial products (meat, leather, wool, hides, etc.); and the repeal of administrative measures regarding the transportation of wine, regulations concerning industrial alcohol, and sanitary regulations concerning colonial products imported by France.

The role of private initiative was strongly emphasized and the creation of professional associations was recommended and encouraged. This dynamism of private initiative was to lead to the creation of new firms and to the continued development of existing concerns. And the professional associations thus constituted were to be able to carry out market surveys and propose their own measures to adjust production and regularize or decrease the costs.

Finally, the conference proposed the creation of a national fund for the public infrastructure of the overseas territories in order to develop the means of transportation necessary for the marketing of colonial goods.[22]

Like the Sarraut Project, the 1935 conference was a failure. Edouard Bonnefous evoked once again financial causes:

> To create or reorganize the economic structures indispensable for the profitability of our colonies, the conference established the equivalent of 800 billion francs as the total of the sums to be invested. No territory, either with its own resources, or through loans could finance its part of such an extensive program. It was necessary to create a special organization, a colonial fund, supported in part by a state subvention. These ideas had to be abandoned because of the difficulties France was experiencing at the time; they were not taken up again until after the war, when the FIDES was created.[23]

It was not until after the Second World War that France could really put into practice the colonial development plans recommended first by the Sarraut Project and subsequently reconsidered and developed in 1935 by the imperial economic conference. The modernization and equipment plans of the French Union were a logical continuation of the Sarraut Project of 1921 and the colonial conference of 1935. But they also took into consideration the recommendations of the Brazzaville Conference of 1944.

The Brazzaville Conference (1944)

The Conference of Brazzaville, which was held from January 30 to February 8, 1944, clearly marked the beginning of a new era in investment policies in Africa. France expressed a commitment "not only to putting her honor on the line, but also to having an interest in having prosperous colonies" because "the access to wealth of everyone who carries the name French is one of the most clear pledges...of the return to greatness."[24] The economic intentions of the French were revealed in a speech made on February 1, 1944, at the launching of the work of the Imperial Economic Commission (*Commission de l'économie impériale*) by Peter who was Inspector of Colonies, Director of Economic Affairs at the Department of the Colonies of the Provisional Government of Alger, and President of the Imperial Economic Commission at Brazzaville. He stated that

> The essential goal we seek in economic matters is the following: a policy of enriching our colonies. What we are striving for is to increase the buying power of the indigenous population which will allow a rise in their living standards.
> We no longer conceive of the economy according to certain private interests, but rather we envision an economy which serves the general interest. This policy is not intended only for Africa. It also has the goal of facilitating the provisioning of the *métropole*. It is clear that France will need a considerable amount of raw materials and that African colonies will have to do their utmost to send them all the resources.
> Thus this development policy does not pursue a purely African goal. It seeks as well to fulfill higher, more long-term goals to contribute to the recovery of the mother country.[25]

After deliberation in a plenary session the conference adopted an important recommendation on economic questions on February 7, 1944. These questions were on "the rationalization of production, especially by the development of mechanization and by the reorganization of the procedures."[26] The principle of industrialization remained within the existing regulations of authorization and control by the public authority. The officials attending the Brazzaville Conference were divided over the important question of industrialization.[27] On this problem the final document to be presented by the *Commissaire aux Colonies* (Head of the Department of Colonies) to the members of the Consultative Assembly was cautious. If industrialization was presented as an element of progress, allowing the buying power of the indigenous population to rise, it should be "pursued in stages with method and prudence, within the strict limits set by the general production plan."[28]

Agricultural development was the second domain to which an investment program was to apply. Finally, there were a series of recommendations practically reiterating both the propositions of the Sarraut Project and the conclusions of the Colonial Conference of 1935: the maintenance and extension of the road network, railway, ports, telecommunications as well as the adaptation of the customs system both to the vicissitudes of the world economy and to the multiple needs of the colonial territories.[29]

In his speech mentioned above, Peter recommended the setting up of a ten-year plan. This FIDES ten-year plan was finally established and adopted in 1946.

NOTES

1. The sections of the French Union are listed under Title VIII of the constitution, articles 60 to 82.
2. The details are contained in a series of decrees dated October 25, 1946 (see *Journal Officiel de la République Française (JORF)*, October 27, 1946, pp. 109–129 and 150). On the creation of the *Assmblée Représentative du Cameroun (ARCAM)*, see *ibid.*, Decree No. 46–2376, and "Rapport Annuel du Gouvernement Français" (1947), pp. 220–226.
3. The details on these conditions can be found in "Rapport Annuel du Gouvernement Français" (1947), p. 14.
4. Joseph (R.), *Le mouvement nationaliste au Cameroun* (Paris: Karthala, 1986), pp. 92–93. The French succeeded in maintaining the double college in Cameroon up until the *Loi Cadre* (outline law) of 1956. Indeed it was this law which in its Article 10 introduced universal suffrage for all political and administrative elections.
5. Cited in "Mission de visite de l'ONU" (1952), p. 10.
6. *Ibid*, p. 37.
7. *Le Cameroun Libre*, 471 (May 1954): 6. See also *Climats*, 440 (May 20–26, 1954): 7.
8. *JORF. Débats de l'Assemblée de l'Union Française* (sessions of July 28 and August 2, 1955).
9. Archives of the United Nations, RAG–2/130/34, file T/PET 5/L.9, "Travaux du 5ème congrès du Kumzse, Association traditionnelle du peuple bamiléké" (Dschang, November 24-30, 1952).
10. "Rapport de la Mission de visite de l'ONU" (1950), p. 59; Archives of the United Nations, DAG–5/2–5–3, file T/PET, 5/L.84 (January 24, 1956).
11. "Mission de visite de l'ONU" (1952), p. 10.

12. It should be noted that in Togo, the other Trust Territory administered by France in Black Africa, like Cameroon, the single college was instituted in 1951.
13. Moreux (R), "Le trusteeship français sur le Cameroun et le Togo," *Marchés Coloniaux* (March 2, 1946): 195.
14. For this text, see "Conseil de Tutelle. Accord de tutelle pour le territoire du Cameroun sous administration française tel qu'il a été approuvé par l'Assemblée Générale le 1er décembre 1946."
15. "Mission de visite de l'ONU" (1949), p. 60.
16. The institution known as *Commissariat Général au Plan*, entrusted to Jean Monnet, was created by decree on January 3, 1946. The Monnet Program was presented in November of the same year. See *L'Année Politique* (1946): 57–62 and 274–277.
17. "Projet de loi portant fixation d'un programme général de mise en valeur des colonies françaises, exposé des motifs," *JORF, Documents Parlementaires, Chambre* (1921): 1574. For details of the project, see *ibid.*, pp. 1574–1662, and Sarraut (A.), *La mise en valeurs des colonies françaises* (Paris: Payot, 1923).
18. The Minister of Colonies gave explicit reasons in his preamble for not incorporating the resources and financial means likely to allow the execution of his program and for putting them separately into a special bill to be submitted subsequently for the approval of Parliament (*JORF, Documents parlementaires*, p. 1574).
19. Jean-François (A), *La France et la mise en valeur de ses colonies* (Paris: Imprimerie des Presses Modernes, 1930), p. 65.
20. Bonnefous (E), *Les milliards qui s'envolent. L'aide française aux pays sous développés* (Paris: Fayard, 1963), p. 19.
21. Hiquily (L), *La Politique impériale et la conférence coloniale de 1935*, p. 136.
22. On all these proposals, see: *Conférence économique de la France métropolitaine et d'outre mer. Rapports généraux et conclusions d'ensemble, T.1 et 2, décembre 1934–avril 1935* (Paris: Larose, 1935); Hiquily (L), pp. 144–149; Ngango (G), *Les investissements d'origine extérieure en Afrique noire francophone: statut et incidences sur le développement* (Paris: Présence Africaine, 1973), pp. 84–86.
23. Bonnefous (E.), p. 23.
24. *La Conférence Africaine Française. Brazzaville. 30 janvier 1944–8 février 1944* (Paris: Ministère des Colonies, 1945), p. 50.
25. ANSOM, affaires économiques 101, "Procès-verbal de la commission de l'économie impériale, 1er février 1944."
26. *La Conférence Africaine Française*, p. 51.
27. On this subject see Marseille (J.), *Empire colonial et capitalisme français. Histoire d'un divorce* (Paris: Albin Michel, 1984), pp. 344–346.
28. ANSOM, affaires économiques 101, "Procès verbal de la commission de l'économie impériale, 7 février 1944."
29. *La Conférence Africaine Française*, pp. 53–55.

Chapter 2

The Organization of FIDES

The Implementation and Mechanisms of FIDES

In the law No. 46–860 of April 30, 1946, the French National Assembly established a long term program for the development and modernization of France's overseas territories entitled *Fonds d'Investissement pour le Développement Economique et Social des Territoires d'Outre Mer* (FIDES). According to Article 1 of this law, the goal of the FIDES Plan was "on the one hand, and primarily to satisfy the needs of the autochthonous population and...on the other hand, in accordance with the plans established by the *Commissariat Général du Plan* (Plan Department) to work towards carrying out the economic reconstruction and development programs of the French Union on the metropolitan level as well as in the area of international trade."[1] The *Commission de Modernisation des Territoires d'Outre Mer* (Committee for the Modernization of Overseas Territories) was charged with drawing up an inventory of not only the resources but also the needs of each individual territory, and with determining the means to be deployed to reach the goals set by the French National Assembly. In 1948 this committee presented its first report which was a veritable charter for a modernization program for French overseas territories.[2]

The first part of the report sets out the general plan of action of FIDES and the means of its execution. This project did not aspire to finalize in a detailed and prescriptive fashion the local programs which were to be determined by the authorities of each territory. It established only a general framework for these authorities and indicated to them the areas in which it was advisable to make a concerted effort as well as the possible magnitude of the projects. Each was to take into account the aid that France could provide for the territory and at the same time coordinate its projects with the plans of the other parts of the French Union. It was also to take into account forecasts about the international economic situation in the years to follow.

The report also established two important principles. The first stipulated that "the franc zone should encompass all of the countries of the Union in order to ensure the completely free movement of capital without exchange restrictions." According to the second principle, "the *métropole* will furnish the majority of the equipment and manufactured goods and the territories will mostly export raw materials." Echoes of the latter principle can be found throughout the programs.

The magnitude of the changes to be accomplished demanded long term planning. A local plan was established for each overseas territory for the period from 1947 to 1957. The assessment of the ten-year program of Cameroon revealed an investment need on the order of 24.7 billion CFA Francs, with 5.2 billion for works of social interest such as urban planning, sanitation, health, education, sport; 1.5 billion for work related to the land including agricultural equipment, forestry, animal husbandry; 1.4 billion for the development of mining, electric energy, industrialization; and finally 16.5 billion for the improvement of the means of ground, sea and air transportation and communication.[3]

The emphasis on improving the infrastructure is clear from the above allocation. Industrialization disappeared from the agenda of the Plan in the course of its implementation. Just as with the Sarraut Plan, the emphasis was placed once again on the need to supply metropolitan France with cheap raw materials and to establish an infrastructure capable of improving the productivity and quick export of agricultural and mining products.

According to Article 2 of the law of April 30, 1946, the Government intended for the preparation and execution of the plan "to orient and coordinate private activities" and "in case of their shortfall to make up for the difference by the creation of state and semi-public firms." This government intervention appeared very clearly from 1948 on, especially in the areas of energy production, credit, insurance, information, mechanical engineering and chemical industries, etc. This led to the creation of a group of state firms and semi-public companies. Among the companies created and set up or working in Cameroon were the following:

State firms

Bureau Minier de la France d'Outre Mer (created by the Decree of January 26, 1948).

Bureau Central d'Etude pour les Equipments d'Outre Mer (created by the Ordinance of February 10, 1949).

Centre Technique Forestier Tropical (created by the Ordinance of June 10, 1949).

Bureau pour le Développement de la Production Agricole dans les Territoires d'Outre Mer (created by the Ordinance of April 29, 1950).
Crédit du Cameroun (created by the Ordinance of May 25, 1949).

Semi-public firms

Compagnie Française pour le Développement des Fibres Textiles (created by the Ordinance of May 19, 1948).
Compagnie Générale des Oléagineux Tropicaux (created by the Ordinance of May 19, 1948).
Energie Electrique du Cameroun (created by the Ordinance of March 3, 1948).
Société Immobilière du Cameroun (created by the Ordinance of July 18, 1952).

Besides releasing the necessary budgetary resources, the implementation of the plan presupposed the creation of institutions capable of assigning these resources and of making use of them outside the regular budgetary rules, as the annual nature of the latter made long term planning difficult. The law of April 30, 1946, anticipated in its Article 3 that the financing of the plans was going to be ensured by an institution named *Fonds d'Investissement pour le Développement Economique et Social des Territoires d'Outre Mer* (FIDES), while Article 5 stipulated that FIDES was going to be managed by an agency called *Caisse Centrale de la France d'Outre mer* (CCFOM). Two decrees, signed on July 5 and October 16, 1946, regulated the organization of FIDES and the special budget by territory or clusters of territories for the execution of the equipment and development plans, respectively.[4]

FIDES was supported in part by a subvention from the French budget the amount of which was set each year by the Finance Law, and in part by the contributions of the concerned territories. Finally, FIDES was supported, again at the expense of the territories, by long term advances (25 years) granted by CCFOM at a low interest rate of 1 percent in principle but 2.2 percent in effect if the "commission" deducted in advance for these operations is taken into consideration.

The decree of June 3, 1949, determined the operational field of FIDES and fixed financing standards,[5] distinguishing between a "general section" financed entirely by state funds (90 percent of the budget, 10 percent in the form of long term advances from CCFOM); and "overseas sections" financed 55 percent from state funds and 45 percent from the local budget[6] funded if needed from advances of CCFOM, repayable in 25 years at 2.2 percent interest. According to Article 3 and 4 of the decree of October 24, 1946, the beginning of the repayment period could be deferred for 5 years from the date of payment.

The general section provided financing for the research necessary for economic and social development, for raising the required capital for state companies, as well as for acquisition of holdings in semi-public companies, and for the realization of projects which by their nature or by their implications were of interest to metropolitan France and several overseas territories. These projects included scientific research, mining and oil research, and major projects of an experimental nature.

The overseas sections financed projects and activities of a local nature. Thus, for example, the large public works projects of the road and port infrastructure and the development of agricultural production, and sanitary and educational infrastructure fell within the purview of these sections. The budgets of these sections were determined jointly by the local assemblies and by the Board of Directors of FIDES. The loans granted could take different forms: advances from FIDES or from CCFOM to public organizations to support the special budgets anticipated by the decree of October 16, 1946,[7] or the provision of the necessary subsidies to state firms or to other public establishments; the participation in semi-public companies; short and medium term loans to private firms at low interest rates.

To escape the burden of annual budgetary votes, which was incompatible with long term planning, and also to escape the rigidity of the old public works programs with borrowed funds setting the goals for several years, the Board of Directors of FIDES, appointed by the French Government, arranged for a permanent delegation of power to the Board by the Parliament, which voted for the loans, leaving to the Board the task of distributing them. This Board of Directors, presided over by the Minister of Overseas France, consisted of three representatives of the concerned ministries, namely Overseas France, Economic Affairs, and Finance; two representatives of the Plan Department; the Director of CCFOM; four members of Parliament; two "technical experts" who were generally the representatives of private monopolies and who were appointed jointly by the Ministers of Overseas France and of the National Economy. The representatives of Parliament, although appointed by the Minister, were in the minority. No representation whatsoever was envisioned for the concerned territories. "This system, made complicated on purpose, managed to avoid all parliamentary control—and all serious public control by means of the pretext of technicalities. It instituted the arbitrary rule of a small group of technocrats and the representatives of private monopolies (often interchangeable) who could dispose of enormous amounts of credits giving priority to the interests of the big businesses which they directly or indirectly represented."[8]

As mentioned earlier the powers of the assembly of Cameroon were limited. However, the case of Cameroon among overseas territories under French rule was not unique, as the following statements shows.

> The local assemblies complained bitterly seeing themselves deprived of their budgetary authority, the forced contributions to the special budgets supported by FIDES were imposed on them without the possibility of discussion and their magnitude restricted their freedom of decision to the minimum—except for increasing taxes to unbearable proportions—in the allocation of the local budget...Even the governors complained about being faced with a *fait accompli* of programs concerning their territories, about which they had not even been consulted![9]

Even official voices denounced "the lack of parliamentary control, the excessive role of *Caisse Centrale*, the irresponsibility of the Board of Directors."[10] As had been the case with the *Fonds d'Emprunts* (Loan Funds) the FIDES loans had to be utilized for purchases within the franc zone, except with special permission, for example, for merchandise unavailable on the French market.

On the fundamental problem of the financing of the Plan, the first report of the *Commission de Modernisation* (Modernization Commission) of the overseas territories noted that they did not have any savings and did not build any. The indigenous populations were using all their income for their immediate consumption needs while the profit made by foreigners was for the most part transferred to France or to foreign countries.[11] In connection with local savings the Blin report of 1951 with regard to private investment in Cameroon was interesting:

> In the countryside of Cameroon there is such a thing as African savings. The Bamileké region is famous in this regard. But these savings do not seem at all likely to move in the near future towards transferable securities, nor towards investment securities in public loans, nor towards savings banks.

This document reports the findings of the French administrators who were working in one of the most important economic regions of the territory, the Bamileké region.

> The Head of the Bamileké region writes: "The Bamileké are essentially thrifty, but their savings are not manifested in the opening of bank accounts or having passbooks but in the purchase of women who for them are sources of new income..." Only some traders invest their savings in the purchase of urban land. It is unlikely, at least in the present state of the social and economic organization of Bamilekéland, that we shall see the appearance of the savings account there.
> As for the Head of the subdivision of Bafoussam, he writes that local savings are

> strong among farmers, and that they appear in the form of an important accumulation and investment in secret commercial companies usually run by parents and friends who are established as traders in the great centers, and that it would be very difficult to bring these savings closer to European style investments or savings banks.
> The Head of the subdivision of Bangangté indicates that savings exist but "not in a liquid form," and that "the most common form of utilization of capital is the pooling of capital and trade is the most frequent form of investment."
> Finally the Head of Bafang declares "all savings in the country are immediately transformed into material goods (construction, plantations, trucks)."

Based on these accounts, the Blin Report makes the following remark on savings in Cameroon:

> In fact we witness a slow evolution of African investment in commercial firms, plantations and construction. But we cannot expect soon the development of a significant savings activity decisively oriented towards investing in holdings of large firms or in public loans.[12]

The execution of the plan could not rely much on local revenue. It was almost entirely subordinated to external contributions. In this respect, the role of the *Caisse Centrale de la France d'Outre Mer* (CCFOM—Central Bank of Overseas France) was of tremendous importance.

CCFOM, which was closely associated with the activities and operation of FIDES, originated from a financial agency known as *Caisse Centrale de la France Libre* which was created in London by the edict of December 1941 to serve as the financial instrument of Free France. Its first objective was to gather the necessary resources for the activities of *Comité de Londres* (the London Committee) and its organs in the territories that had sided with the government of Free France. In addition, it was the financial institution that issued currencies for French Equatorial Africa and Cameroon where the banknotes and coins remaining under the control of Vichy issued by *Banque de l'Afrique Occidentale* (Bank of West Africa) were in circulation. After it became *Caisse Centrale de la France d'Outre Mer* (CCFOM) it conserved its special role as the financial institution to issue currencies in the territories hitherto controlled by Free France, namely French Equatorial Africa and Cameroon, and became a credit institution incorporated into the mechanisms of FIDES.

CCFOM's own operations were those that were likely to depend on bank financing. Thus, CCFOM played the role of a bank by providing support to communes, to state or semi-public firms, and to private companies or firms with a view to allowing or facilitating the financing of operations likely to contribute to the economic and social development of the overseas territories, such as urban development, the construction of housing, the production and consumption of electric energy, and the establishment of existing industries.

The modalities of the support granted by CCFOM ranged from interest-bearing loans of short, medium or long term to the acquisition of holdings of companies to the simple granting of rediscount facilities. The interest rate of the loans was variable, ranging between 3 and 7 percent. It could be fixed or progressive, depending on the nature of the operation to be financed.

For a long time the issuing banks played the role of deposit and investment banks. It was possible to obtain credit from issuing houses without a private banker intervening. The overseas issuing houses could thus compete with commercial banks. Although its charter authorized it to carry out all operations performed by the issuing houses which it replaced, CCFOM, which had no direct relationship with clients, confined itself primarily to being the "bank of banks."

Before 1945 the private banking network consisted of institutions whose role and significance were strictly local. The metropolitan banks were represented only by a very few branches. After the war, however, their number grew in Black Africa. Table 2.1 shows the development of the banking network in Cameroon from 1939 to 1955. The increase in the number of French banks during this period is quite obvious. The number rose from two in 1939 to four in 1945, to reach eighteen by 1955. During the same period only a single non-French bank appears to have been operating in the territory; that was the British Bank of West Africa.

The different commercial banks supported firms established in Cameroon. They exercised short, medium and long term banking operations. There were also a number of credit agencies specialized in medium or long term operations. Credits were granted to firms and commercial companies as well as to planters. Among these credit institutions were *Crédit de l'AEF*, *Crédit du Cameroun*, *Crédit Foncier de l'Ouest Africain*, *Société d'Etudes et de Gestion de l'Afrique Noire*, *Société Immobilière et Financière Africaine*, and *Société Financière pour le Développement du Cameroun*.

The Beginnings of FIDES in Cameroon

Before discussing the era of the Plan which began in 1946, it is necessary to first evoke the situation in Cameroon during the immediate post-war period. This was a troubled period characterized by economic and social malaise. An interesting example was the Mungo region where there was agitation caused by several factors. Before and during the war the principal cash crop of the region was bananas. An increasing number of Cameroonians of this region, especially the Bamileké, some Duala, and some of the indigenous population,

Table 2.1

The development of the banking network in Cameroon from 1939 to 1955

Banks	Headquarters	12–31–1939	12–31–1945	12–31–1955
Banque Nationale pour le Commerce et l'Industrie (1)	Paris		1	5
Société Générale (2)	Paris			2
Crédit Lyonnais (3)	Paris			4
Banque de l'Afrique Occidentale (4)	Paris	1	1	4
Banque Commerciale Africaine (5)	Paris	1	2	3
British Bank of West Africa (6)	London	1	1	1

Source: adapted from Bloch-Lainé (F), *La zone franc* (Paris: PUF, 1956), p. 228.

(1) Established in Douala (October 1944), Yaoundé (January 1947), Nkongsamba (July 1948), and Garoua (February 1951).
(2) Established in Douala (October 1947).
(3) Established in Douala (November 1946), and Yaoundé (May 1947).
(4) Established in Douala (1928) and Yaoundé (November 1949).
(5) Established in Douala (1925) and Yaoundé (1944).
(6) Established in Douala (1925), its clientele consisted essentially of the important English trading companies established in Cameroon.

adopted cash-cropping. However, they were excluded from the banana production for export until 1946. "African planters see for the most part with increasing discontent (that) the profits of the banana culture totally elude them. This situation and the abuses which it entailed during the war were to have serious political consequences."[13]

From 1932 to 1940, even though the land was available the banana economy's peculiar structures reserved this lucrative activity for Europeans. Organizations included, on the Cameroonian side, the *Syndicat de Défense des Intérêts Bananiers* and the *Union Bananière du Cameroun*, and on the commercial side *Martin Frères* and later the *Compagnie des Bananes* affiliated with the Anglo-American Trust, Elders and Fyffes Ltd.[14] After 1940 the war effort was no longer simply used as a pretext for forcing thousands of Cameroonians to work on the European plantations, but just as significantly, many Cameroonian planters were obliged to neglect or abandon their plantations in order to provide the labor required of them on the European plantations.[15]

Unlike Europeans, Cameroonians only had the *Sociétés Indigènes de Prévoyance* (SIP) to organize their economic interests. These organizations were essentially inefficient. Their origins go back to the *commissions agricoles* of 1923, and to the *mutuelles agricoles et d'élévage* of 1925, which were more developed and from which the SIPs derived. These organizations were intended to assist rural Cameroonians in agricultural matters, but it was precisely these rural Cameroonians who were the most opposed to them. These organizations were perceived to be paternalistic and anti-democratic because the French administrators played a dominant role in their functioning. People were obliged to pay a special tax to support this functioning but had no say in how the money was spent. And finally, villagers had no choice as to whether they wished to join or not, which went against the cooperative spirit that these organizations were supposed to foster.[16] After the war, nonetheless, the Mungo area and also the Bamileké and Bamoun regions saw the emergence of a wave of enthusiasm among Cameroonians to create their own autonomous cooperatives whose motivations were as much political as economic.[17]

While the SIPs run by French administrators had been primarily concerned with providing agricultural supplies and equipment, the Cameroonians themselves concentrated more closely on the marketing of their products. This development was not merely imitation, it also constituted a reaction against the economic domination achieved by the *colons* (settlers) thanks to their trade unions and to the close links their groups had with internationally important firms. Many Duala owned land in the Mungo region. Some had been driven out by the crisis of 1930 and few were able to overcome the difficulties faced by Cameroonians in working their lands in this region during the war. The Duala were able to articulate the grievances of a particular group of Cameroonians, in this case the planters of the Mungo who had not yet organized itself to defend its interests, as it was to do after the war.

Even if the economic and social unrest among the Duala in many ways was less severe than in the rural zones, the urban unrest was largely the consequence of earlier developments in the countryside. One of the direct consequences of the forced labor imposed upon Cameroonians during the war was their massive exodus from the countryside to the towns. The Mungo, Nyong and Sanaga, and Sanaga Maritime regions where the great majority of the European plantations were found were particularly affected by forced labor. The frequent use of *indigénat*, a judicial system utilized to administer local indigenes in Cameroon, and forced labor by the colonial administration during the war arguably led to the most important wave of emigration of Cameroonians to Douala. The town grew at a faster rate than in the previous twenty-five years.[18] The problems that emerged in Douala were thus in part the result of rural problems transferred to the town.

Most problems related to the rapid urbanization of Southern Cameroon already existed by 1944–45. One of them was the rapid population growth, to the point that by 1944 the indigenous Duala were already most likely a minority in their own town. Many of the newcomers were unemployed or under employed in the countryside and many of them were to remain that way because of the slow rate of economic growth in the immediate postwar period. This delay was in part due to lack of infrastructure in the territory after twenty-five years of French rule.

Just as in many other parts of the world directly affected by the war, Cameroonians had to put up with shortages of essential goods. The shortages of imported goods, as well as the manpower requirements occasioned by the "war effort," were two ills which weighed particularly heavily on the populations of the South. Since 1935, these populations had become regular consumers of all those goods that were lacking during the war years, such as sugar, cloth, construction materials, tools, and equipment, and were little inclined to accept salaried work especially as the stores were empty. The cocoa and coffee planters had other problems. Their crops which were constantly increasing in size before the war could not find buyers. In 1943 and 1944 tons of coffee and cocoa were burnt in Douala and Ebolowa.

Urban Cameroonians not only suffered from the inconveniences of wartime but also from the peculiar nature of the economy which was increasingly dominated by the *colons* during the war. The strengthening of the economic power of the *colons* had two direct consequences for urban Cameroonians, namely the maintenance of low wages and a considerable rise in prices due to the artificial wartime prosperity.

It might be worthwhile asking the question whether the nascent Cameroonian bourgeoisie, who adopted a European lifestyle suffered more from the higher prices and rationing than the working class. It is estimated that the price hikes reduced to nothing the gains in salary that the civil servants had obtained since 1937 and that in 1944 the buying power of an agricultural laborer in Douala was half of what it had been in 1938.[19]

Thus, while North Cameroon remained isolated and particularistic, the entire south of the country seemed to be profoundly marked by the economic consequences of the war, much more so than the other French territories which had not become modernized to the same extent. Towards the end of the war the internal economic unrest of the territory was primarily expressed in the organization of trade unions. With the coming of a plan whose primary objective was to satisfy the needs of the autochthonous population, an improvement of the situation could be expected. Unfortunately this was not immediately the case due to the slowness of the implementation of the Plan. In early 1948 deputy Dr. Ajoulat observed:

> Practically since its creation, the activities of the FIDES were taken up with the examination of the files provided by the territories, research institutions or private firms with a view to obtaining subventions or advances. At no point was it possible for the committee to come to a decision on the plans or the programs in their totality.[20]

And later, Ebédé who was a member of the ARCAM, complained during a meeting of this assembly held on October 19, 1949 by saying that "You are aware that since 1946 they speak to us of a plan of equipment. I note that until now nothing had been done." The representative of the government responded:

> You demand immediate action! You know that France has just suffered ten years of war and occupation, and during this time she did not hesitate to undertake a program of development for this territory. The French taxpayer has made a considerable effort, and if for three years the achievements are not as obvious as you would wish it is because preliminary studies are needed; we met with all kinds of material difficulties; studies of this kind cannot be accomplished in 24 hours. They are now more or less completed for the overall project design and we are entering the phase of implementation. I beg you then to be patient for another year or two.[21]

Regarding the question of the implementation of the ten year plan a report made by High Commissioner André Soucadaux can also be evoked. In a speech given on the occasion of the opening of the extraordinary session of ARCAM in January 1950 Soucadaux acknowledged that "the pace of the execution of the works and supplies did not, until 1949, follow the rhythm of the programs and the opening of credit." According to him, the reasons for this were: "too few public works projects established in the territory; weakness in a number of metropolitan industries; lack of external means of payment during the initial years."[22]

The slowness of the execution of the plan did not preclude the injection of French capital into the Cameroonian economy during the first three years of the Plan. The most important source of this capital was FIDES. Table 5.8 shows the payments made by this agency, and table 5.9 provides the amounts of investment in Cameroon financed by CCFOM which was the second main source of French capital (see chapter 5). These numbers indicate that the investments of FIDES increased from 162 million CFA Francs in 1947, to 655 million in 1948, and to 1,801 million in 1949, while those of CCFOM were 80 million in 1947, 64 million in 1948, and 135 million in 1949. The third source of French capital was constituted by the state budget. From 1946 to 1949, spending from this budget for the territory (see table 5.12 in chapter 5) was 7 million CFA in 1946, 8 million in 1947, 32 million in 1948, and 10 million in 1949. This state investment was exclusively dedicated to aviation infrastructure.

To all this needs to be added the credit accorded by the Marshall Plan. Preceded by the Blum-Byrnes agreements of 1946, then by the "intermediate aid" of November 1947 which affected consumer goods only and excluded equipment, the Marshall Plan voted by the American Congress on April 3, 1948, and in effect until July 1, 1952 had as its official goal to aid in the reconstruction of Europe. The supplies granted to Europe were to be paid for in local currency, and this "counter-value" remained at the disposal of the American government to be used eventually for financing local investment in agreement with the interested governments.

The counter-value in francs of the aid given by the Marshall Plan to the French Union served in part to finance equipment programs in the new departments and territories that were under the purview of the Ministry of Overseas France. It was thus that for Cameroon the "Marshall dollars," whose amount rose (in thousands of dollars) from 3,162 in 1948 to 6,861.5 in 1949, were utilized for important road construction work, the modernization of the railway network of the territory, and for significant works on the port of Douala.[23] These loans constituted only one part, but nonetheless an important one of the currency allocated for the equipment of the territory. Table 2.2 shows the totality of loans in foreign currency utilized for equipment in Cameroon from January 1, 1947 to October 15, 1949.

Table 2.2

Credit in foreign exchange allocated to Cameroon for its equipment from January 1, 1947 to October 15, 1949 (amounts in dollars)

Marshall Plan	4,238,729
Loans in Pound Sterling	9,247,195
Loans in dollars	6,490,000
Other currencies	4,150,000
TOTAL	24,125,924

Source: Adapted from "Cameroun français. Budget des recettes et des dépenses, exercice 1950" (Yaoundé: Imprimerie du gouvernement, 1950), p. 10.

> The influence of the franc zone on the monetary plane seems to be favorable in several respects. France guarantees the Cameroonian money. France brings its monetary support in the case of a deficit in the balance of payments. The free transfer and convertibility of currencies facilitates exchanges between Cameroon and the other countries of the franc zone and the influx of public capital to Cameroon. Nevertheless, several less favorable aspects need to be mentioned: because the CFA franc is linked to the French franc by a fixed exchange rate the devaluation of the latter means an automatic devaluation to the same degree as the satellite currencies...The monetary zone facilitates the repatriation of private funds towards the *métropole*. And finally the zone greatly influences Cameroon's external trade.[25]

The freedom of transfers helped not only capital flight but also the flow of money from the dominant economy. One of the major consequences of the influx of French capital to Cameroon during the first years of the plan was the growth of the money supply in the territory. According to the figures given by the French Government, the total of the means of payment in Cameroon, including fiduciary circulation and private credit accounts, rose from about 1,793 CFA Francs in 1947 to 3,666 in 1948 and to about 4,573 in 1949.[26]

The inflation ran the risk of influencing prices, if the liquid assets were not absorbed by consumption of goods. Following the end of the war, from an economic point of view, Cameroon found itself in a transitional period which was characterized by shortages in the supply of imported goods. From 1940 on, the territory continuously received a relative abundance of consumer goods from the Allies. With the end of the war these Allied supplies began to gradually diminish. This was partly due to the fact that the enormous demand in the liberated territories led the Allies to re-orient the flow of goods—which had hitherto been directed towards Africa—towards Europe and Asia. In addition, the limitations in foreign exchange credit accorded to Cameroon obliged it to limit its purchases abroad. Metropolitan France, that was still waiting for her production levels to increase, could only deliver a limited amount of supplies to the territory until the end of the 1940s. As a result, the Cameroonian economy in the first years following the war suffered a serious setback due to insufficiencies in imports.[27] Table 2.4 shows the development of the value of exports from and imports to Cameroon from 1946 to 1948, and also illustrates the place of France in the foreign trade of the territory in this period.

With regard to Cameroonian exports, the share of France rose from about 53 percent in 1946 to 68 percent in 1947 and to 75 percent in 1948, while the territory's exports increased from 16 percent in 1946 to 47 percent in 1947 and 67 percent in 1948. It is also to be noted that until 1947 there was a positive balance of trade with France and it only began to become negative in 1949 with the beginning of the Plan.

Table 2.4

The development of Cameroon's imports and exports from 1946 to 1948 (amounts in CFA Francs)

	Exports		Imports	
Years	Total	France	Total	France
1946	1,210.6	542.6	1,004.2	163
1947	1,631.8	1,105.5	2,197.0	1,041
1948	4,285.5	3,217.9	4,888.1	3,263.7

Source: "Commerce extérieur du Cameroun oriental, 1946-1956" (Yaoundé: Présidence de la République).

This surplus indicates above all a much more considerable increase in the prices of imported goods than in those of exported products. In 1946 the price of the goods Cameroon bought abroad saw a 40 percent increase in part due to the devaluation of December 1945.[28] Furthermore, in many cases the supplying countries themselves raised the prices of their goods due to the rise in their cost price.

Moreover, although the separation of the colonial franc from the metropolitan franc lessened the difference in the existing prices between the metropolitan and the local economy, the cost of French merchandise remained in general much higher than that of non-French products. Pierre Mayère, editor in chief of *Climats*, called attention to this difference between French and world prices:

> What to say of the French trucks, which at the end of the day cost three times as much as the American vehicles, which are stronger and better adapted to transportation on bush roads!
> It is this difference between the French and the other world prices which provoke in Cameroon this general push towards economic if not political autonomy. That is because the *métropole* pretends to buy Cameroonian products at world prices. But by not providing Cameroon the currencies which it needs for its exports, it obliges this territory to buy French merchandise at prices which are well over those of the world market.[29]

Commenting further on the question of the goods imported by the territory Pierre Fouletier, president of ARCAM at the time, remarked during the ordinary session of this assembly in September 1949, that these goods were "too expensive...of inferior quality" and that many of them did not meet "the needs and tastes of the consumers."[30]

As far as export goods were concerned, the outcome of the adjustment to world prices decided upon in early 1946 by the French following the devaluation of December 1945 was a rise of between 10 and 60 percent of almost all export goods.[31] A considerable growth in the money supply in circulation was to be expected, which was to weigh heavily on the local prices. A rise in salaries inevitably followed that of the prices of commodities and products.[32]

Towards 1948–1949, the territory suffered from various imbalances, such as the differences between the salaries, the price of imported goods, and those of exported products. There was a general rise in the cost of living provoked by the shortage of some goods and especially by the rise in the price of imported goods. This rise in prices at the end of the 1940s constituted one of the main socio-economic hardships in Cameroon. The trusts, and also the French Administration were blamed for this situation. The *Monde Nouveau*, a local newspaper, noted:

> The people responsible for running our economy are incapable of stopping the rise in the cost of living because they are afraid of the trusts, not to mention the fact that they do not dare to go against those to whom they probably owe certain obligations.
> It is to be noted that the trusts are the suppliers of the black market because the administration had given these large houses a monopoly on imports by giving them very high currency quotas based on the fact that they had had export priorities from before the war. If the currency has been given to the new African and European importers, the latter would have brought the goods to our markets at competitive prices that would have lowered prices.
> (Leaving) high importation quotas to these large houses means perpetuating the same problems of the rise in the cost of living which goes hand in hand with a rise in salaries. This vicious cycle must end.[33]

Another imbalance was the overabundance of the money supply in circulation and the lack of imported goods. In 1949, the French Government itself acknowledged this when it wrote in its report to the United Nations Organization on Cameroon that

> The world prices favoring exports, the euphoria of loans putting an increased volume of the means of payment on the market, the launching of the ten year plan of equipment brought…to the territory a significant amount of credit while at the same time the importation of consumer goods remained clearly insufficient.[34]

High Commissioner René Hoffher was of the opinion that the money supply at the disposal of autochthones outstripped their possibilities for purchases.[35] The money supply in the hands of the autochthones could not be absorbed by imported goods. He also indicated that Cameroon suffered from a lack of cloth, of food products, etc.

Until 1949–1950 African economies in general remained dominated by the shortages inherited from the war. Quotas and rationing persisted in all domains. In 1946, the volume of imports was 20 percent less than that of 1938 in Cameroon; whereas the reduction in imports from 1940 to 1945 due to the war and the need for massive renewal of equipment which was on its last legs called for the reestablishment of a normal situation which would have meant a volume of imports well exceeding that of before the war. Although this level was achieved in 1947–1948, the shortages continued.[36]

Under the pretext of protecting the colonies which had then to draw on foreign monetary zones, especially the dollar, for the bulk of their imports the decree of December 25, 1945 created the CFA franc. This was done because France—which had just barely risen from the war—was incapable of meeting these needs. The CFA franc was created partially to avoid the devaluations of the post-war years. Its initial value, set at 1.7 metropolitan francs, was changed to 2 francs on October 17, 1948. This rate was maintained for the rest of the period under consideration in this study. The devaluation of January 1948 contributed not only to inflation but also to public expenditures and to an influx of capital for which the change of the CFA franc from 1.7 to 2 French Francs on October 17, 1948 was a considerable bonus.

The influx of French capital to Cameroon during the first years of the Plan also created imbalances which further complicated an already troubled socio-economic situation. When it was adopted, the Plan did not merely address economic preoccupations such as the re-establishment and development of the productive capacities of the colonial territories with the goal of meeting the pressing and growing needs of Metropolitan France. There were also considerations of a political order. In its editorial of June 15, 1946, *Marchés Coloniaux* underlined the close connection between the design of the Plan and reforms following the laws of April 11, 1946 which abolished forced labor; of May 7, 1946, conferring citizenship on the former "subjects"; and of May 9, 1946 on the organization and the competence of the local assemblies.

Even if the principles behind the abolition of forced labor and of the extension of citizenship were not questioned, an attempt was made from the end of 1946 on to limit the effects of those laws and even to return to the old colonial practices. The integral change in the old methods and the technical renewal anticipated in 1946 presupposed a massive investment effort for which the means had to be made available beforehand. By comparison to the daring plans of 1946 the effort began slowly and incompletely.

In early 1950, the report of the Plan Department on overseas equipment adjusted the forecast of the "Ten-Year Plan." A decree issued on December 11, 1951 reduced the duration of the Plan from ten to four years and substituted two Four-Year Plans for the Ten-Year Plan.

NOTES

1. *JORF, lois et décrets* (May 1, 1946): 3655.
2. "Commissariat Général du Plan de Modernisation et d'Equipement. Premier rapport de Commission de Modernisation des Territoires d'Outre Mer" (January 1, 1948), part 1.
3. Archives de l'Institut Charles de Gaulle (Archives of the Charles de Gaulle Institute, Paris), AICDG, carton 61, "Cameroun" (Ministère de la France d'Outre Mer). It is to be noted that the value of one CFA franc CFA was 1.70 French francs in 1946 and 1947, 1.76 in 1948, and 2 for the rest of the period concerning this study.
4. See *JORF, Lois et Décrets*, 164 (July 14, 1946): 6377; and 244 (October 18, 1946): 8862.
5. See *JORF, Lois et Décrets*, 133 (June 4, 1949): 5481.
6. This proportion became 75 percent in 1954, and then—at least in the case of production and social equipment—100 percent starting in 1956.
7. See *JORF, Lois et Décrets*, 244 (October 18, 1946): 8862.
8. Suret-Canale (J.), *Afrique noire occidentale et centrale, T3, De la décolonisation aux indépendances, 1945–1960, vol.1, Crise du système colonial et capitalisme monopoliste d'Etat* (Paris: Editions Sociales, 1977), p.106.
9. *Ibid.*
10. Denivat (P), "La réforme du FIDES," *Marchés Coloniaux*, 132 (May 22, 1948): 789–792.
11. "Commissariat Général du Plan," p. 44.
12. ANSOM, affaires économiques 85, "Investissements privés," Rapport Blin.
13. Cornevin (R.), *Histoire de l'Afrique, T3, colonisation, décolonisation, indépendance* (Paris:Payot, 1975), p. 590.
14. *Climats*, 2 (July 1953): 51.
15. Edoo (P.), cited by Joseph (R), p. 70.
16. "La gestion de la France au Cameroun", *Notes et Etudes Documentaires*, 1365 (August 8, 1950): 22–23).
17. Joseph (R.), p. 71.
18. It is estimated that there were 25,000 Cameroonians in Douala in 1914 and 40,000 in 1939. From 1939 to 1945, the population increased by 20,000 and reached 60,000 in 1945. The abolition of the *laissez-passer* in May 1946, an administrative document formerly required of all Cameroonians who wished to move from one administrative district to another, only increased emigration to the towns. (R. Joseph, p. 72).
19. Joseph (R.), p. 73.
20. *Marchés Coloniaux*, 116 (January 31, 1948): 61.
21. *JOCF, ARCAM, Procès verbaux des séances*, 25th ordinary session, September 30– October 30, 1949, session of October 19, 1949 (Yaoundé: Imprimerie du gouvernement), p. 15.
22. *JOCF, ARCAM*. Extraordinary session, January 16– February 28, 1950, p. 50.
23. "Aspects financiers et budgétaires du développement économique des territoires d'outre mer," *Chronique d'Outre Mer*, 10 (November 1951): 13. From December 25, 1945, the exchange rate of the dollar was fixed at 70 CFA Francs.
24. *Marchés Coloniaux*, 161 (December 11, 1948): 2209.
25. Hugon (P.), *Analyse du sous développement en Afrique noire. L'exemple de l'économie du Cameroun* (Paris: PUF, 1968), p. 151.
26. "Rapport Annuel du Gouvernement Français" (1952), p. 66.
27. "Cameroun français. Budget" (1947), p. 3.
28. *Ibid.*, p. 5.

29. Mayère, (P.), "Sur les routes du Cameroun," *Climats,* 124 (April 28, 1948): 3. See also *Climats,* 127 (May 19, 1948).
30. *JOCF, ARCAM* (September 30, 1949): 15.
31. "Cameroun Français. Budget" (1947), p. 5. From the end of 1945 to September 1946, the price of robusta coffee rose from 17,000 to 28,000 CFA Francs, that of arabica coffee from 18,400 to 38,000, that of palm kernels from 3,500 to 7,000 and that of palm oil from 6,000 to 12,330. The price paid to the cocoa producers almost doubled. *Ibid.*
32. *Ibid.* and *JOCF, ARCAM*, session of March 31 to April 14, 1949, p. 19.
33. *Monde Nouveau,* 5 (April 1, 1949): 5– 6.
34. "Rapport Annuel du Gouvernement Français" (1949), p. 43.
35. "Diagnostic du Cameroun," *Bulletin de la France d'Outre Mer*, 1 (January 1949): p. 7.
36. Suret-Canale (J.), p. 81.

Chapter 3

The FIDES First Four-Year Plan (1949–1953)

The General Situation

The Polarization of Cameroonian Politics

As Dieudonné Oyono demonstrated in his work, *"La politique africaine du Cameroun,"*[1] the term of André Soucadaux who served as High Commissioner of France in Cameroon from 1949 to 1953 was marked by ambiguities and misunderstandings. These led to two dualistic and asymmetrical discourses. On the one hand, the UPC presented its activity as a crusade against France's diversion of her UNO mission to the old colonial aims. The UPC also called upon Cameroonians to pronounce themselves for or against the French policy, which it represented as being contrary to the trusteeship agreement, aimed at leading the territory to independence. On the other hand, the French Administration in Cameroon depicted the UPC as a representative of international communism. In the climate of the Cold War the Administration also required the Cameroonian populations to take sides, for or against "the communist peril" in Cameroon. Thus, the support that these two extremes of the Cameroonian political spectrum received from the populations of the territory at the beginning of the 1950s was based on a dual misunderstanding which in turn explains the polarized and asymmetric nature of their respective political alliances.

Um Nyobè presented the creation of the UPC as a battle for the liberty and dignity of Cameroonians against the misdeeds of French policy. His vision of the Cameroonian political scene was dualistic. He divided the field of social actors into "oppressors" and "oppressed." To overcome this situation, which he deemed morally wrong, he called into question French policy in its entirety.

Faced with the rise of the UPC, between 1949 and 1953 High Commissioner André Soucadaux, on behalf of the Administration, formulated a response in a joint effort with Dr. Louis Paul Aujoulat, a resident Frenchman who was at that time Deputy of Cameroon and Secretary of State for Overseas France. The two men set out to curtail the influence of the UPC, and to this end argued that it was affiliated with the international communist movement. From the beginning of the 1950s there was a proliferation of political parties in Cameroon. Their creation was supported by the Administration, and they were for the most part fervently opposed to the UPC.

The UPC was defeated in the elections for the French National Assembly in June 1951, and for ATCAM in 1952. After this ballot defeat, the principal problem facing the UPC and the Administration was one of a rift in communication. On the one side, the French Administration was freshly strengthened by the victory of its allies for whom these elections constituted a test of legitimacy. On the other side, the UPC accused the electoral system, engineered by France for its overseas territories, of excluding from the consultations the UPC's natural supporters, the popular masses.[2] The fact that the composition of the electorate was based on educational achievement and wealth gave credence to this charge.

From that time on, the UPC and the Administration no longer really engaged each other in meaningful dialogue. They only addressed themselves to possible third parties or to their own constituencies. Rather than trying to bring their political adversaries to adopt a more constructive stance, both urged internal and international public opinion to take sides. The debates of the Fourth Committee of the General Assembly of the UN in December 1952 and the repercussions they had in Cameroon serve as illustration.[3] Without communication there is no negotiation. The political debate focused on these entrenched positions and the parties involved became deadlocked. The more the two extremes of the Cameroonian political scene tried to convince the adverse party of the justice of their respective causes the more they became radicalized. Thus the political debate was transformed into a question of pride, which made any possibility of political cohabitation difficult. The rift came about during the term of Roland Pré, who succeeded André Soucadaux in 1954 as High Commissioner in Cameroon. It demonstrated that while the debate remained bogged down there was little chance of arriving at a compromise.

Prior to this rift, a certain measure of political calm was favorable to the influx of both private and public capital to Cameroon, especially from 1949 to 1953. This led to what could be viewed as an economic "boom."

Private Capitalism and the General Situation

The intensification of the colonial exploitation of French Tropical Africa was largely determined by the French and the international economic and political situation. As in the aftermath of the First World War, the economic position of French imperialism, and this time also France's political standing, had been seriously shaken. Consequently, the French looked for new sources of profit in this part of their empire, which until then had remained mostly untapped. The recovery of the metropolitan economy, the contraction of the capitalist world market (its loss of influence in central and eastern Europe), and the collapse of the colonial system in Asia encouraged increasing interest in the as yet untapped wealth of Black Africa. This "entrenchment" in Africa had other strategic underpinnings as well.

Until the end of the 1940s, African economies remained dominated by the shortages inherited from the war. Export-import quotas and rationing persisted in all areas of the economy. The establishment of export-import quotas transformed the de facto monopolies into "legal" monopolies: the so called *régime des antériorités* allocated import licenses to commercial houses, primarily based on the proportion of their respective import activities in the years just before the war.[4]

The recession of 1949 had little impact on the French African market, which was tied to France where the shortages had not yet been overcome, and was still essentially subject to taxation. By contrast, the recovery and the "boom" of 1950–1951, following the Korean War, were strongly felt and their impact was heightened because of political reasons. On this subject one observer noted that

> It seems to me that a shift in metropolitan interests towards Black Africa is not unrelated to the fear of a war between the United States and Russia.
> Here as in Washington, a hypothetical future conflict is envisioned along the same schema. It is thought that under circumstances or conditions as yet ill defined, the Russians would occupy Europe and that Africa would receive immediate support from the Americans. Capital is being hastily invested primarily in the most profitable sector, that of construction.
> This phenomenon is not only to be found in Dakar, but in the whole of French West Africa.[5]

French Equatorial Africa and Cameroon, and especially such cities as Brazzaville and Douala, did not escape this phenomenon.

The economic boom of 1950–1951 can also be explained by the organizational needs identified by the Plan with respect to the economic development of the territory in two areas: that of production and especially of engineering equipment. From 1949 in Cameroon, this reorganization resulted in the expansion of the banking system, the establishment of trading companies specializing in heavy equipment, the setting up of important French public works and road repairs firms, the establishment of the first public-private partnerships (such as ENELCAM, which was entrusted with the building of the hydroelectric complex of Edéa), and an increase in private capital investment. A report by the French authorities estimated that from 1947 to 1953 this private investment amounted to 18 billion CFA Francs, of which 10 billion went to traditional agricultural production, and 7.5 billion to new ventures in the agricultural, industrial and commercial sectors.[6]

With the failure of colonial aspirations elsewhere, such as in Indochina, Cameroon became the favored target of investors. With its multiple resources Cameroon inspired confidence; it even became a refuge for available capital. High Commissioner André Soucadaux forcefully expressed this point of view when he stated that

> Attracted by the solidity of the economic structure and by the political calm of the territory, significant metropolitan capital is rushing to Cameroon. Consequently, in Douala alone investments of two billion CFA were made in 1951.
> The large firms transferred from Indochina are interested in establishing large palm oil and rubber plantations in Cameroon alongside with the already existing ones.[7]

According to Huguette Durand, 369 new companies were created in French Black Africa in 1951 and the increase in the capital of the existing firms attained its highest level.[8] Documents published by the statistical service of the Ministry of Overseas France give different figures, which nonetheless confirm the boom of 1951. Table 3.1 shows new companies and those that increased the volume of their capital in Cameroon and in Black Africa from 1949 to 1953.

Public Capitalism and the General Situation

The influx of capital did not involve the private domain only. Large amounts of metropolitan capital from the public sector also arrived in the territory. The First Four-Year Plan was adopted not long before it was to be completed. The overlap between the two plans makes it difficult to provide an accurate assessment of the sums expended. "The implementation of the first plan, halted beginning in 1953, makes provisions for the granting of credit payments until 1955 and for effective payments until 1956."[9]

The most important source of French public capital reaching Cameroon from 1950 to 1953 was FIDES. The transfers made by this organization appear in table 5.8 (see chapter 5). The numbers in this table indicate that the credit extended to Cameroon amounted to about 3,241 million CFA Francs in 1950, 4,399 million in 1951, 5,364 million in 1952, and 4,420 million in 1953. During the same period numerous loans were also granted to Cameroon by

Table 3.1

New companies and companies increasing their capital investment in Cameroon and Black Africa from 1949 to 1953 (N: number; C: capital in millions of CFA Francs)

Year	Creation of new firms	Increasing of capital	Total for Cameroon	Total for Africa
1949	N: 41	N: 21	N: 62	N: 450
	C: 91.6	C: 277.6	C: 369.2	C: 3,739.6
1950	N: 78	N: 30	N: 108	N: 511
	C: 334	C: 434.4	C: 768.4	C: 4,345.1
1951	N: 94	N: 48	N: 142	N: 534
	C: 770.2	C: 822.3	C: 1,592.5	C: 6,343.9
1952	N: 92	N: 44	N: 136	N: 462
	C: 399.7	C: 1,069.3	C: 1,469	C: 5,844.4
1953	N: 91	N: 43	N: 134	N: 510
	C: 145.3	C: 869.4	C: 1,041,7	C: 4,912.3

Source: Adapted from Atangana (M), "French Capitalism and Nationalism in Cameroon", *African Studies Review*, 40, No 1 (April 1997): 93.

CCFOM. The amount of these loans, shown in table 5.9, was about 750 million CFA Francs in 1950, 1,071 million in 1951, 1,694 million in 1952, and 1,907 million in 1953. Finally, the sums allocated to Cameroon from the French national budget amounted to 16 million CFA Francs in 1950, 103 million in 1951, 197 million in 1952, and 270 million in 1953 (see table 5.12, chapter 5).

The expansion of French capitalism during the period of the First Plan led to a significant growth in the money supply in Cameroon. According to the French annual report on Cameroon to the UN, the total amount of the means of payment in the territory which amounted to about 4,500.0 million CFA Francs in 1949 rose to 6,244.8 million in 1950, 7,344.3 million in 1951, 9,245.6 million in 1952, and reached 11,130 million in 1953.[10]

The public financing of French investment in Cameroon created obligations for the territory. The repayment of non-FIDES CCFOM loans by local administrations and local public firms during the period of the First Plan were made in 1951, 1952 and 1953. These repayments which are presented in table 5.3 (see chapter 5) amounted to 2.3 million CFA Francs in 1951, 6.3 million in 1952, and 8.6 million in 1953.

Table 3.2

Allocations of Cameroon's budget for debt service and contributions of the territory to the functioning of French agencies from 1950 to 1953 (amounts in CFA Francs)

	1950	1951	1952	1953
Annual loans repayments	2,596,000	3,030,000	7,852,000	10,712,000
Amortization & Interests of FIDES loans	(N/A)	100,000,000	100,000,000	284,356,000
Contributions of the Territory	27,631,300	33,428,300	69,232,000	7,000,000
TOTAL	30,227,300	136,458,300	177,084,000	302,068,000

Source: "Cameroun français. Budget."

Concerning FIDES, although no direct participation of Cameroon is noted, there are some figures regarding its repayments of CCFOM loans. According to a study carried out by the researchers of IEDES, these repayments amounted to 5.4 million CFA Francs in 1952 alone.[11] An examination of the budgets of Cameroon makes it possible to determine the sums dedicated by the territory to annual repayments on loans, amortization and interest repayments of loans agreed to by FIDES, as well as the contribution of Cameroon to numerous French agencies, a list of which has already been provided (see chapter 2). Table 3.2 shows these sums for the duration of the First Four-Year Plan.

Evaluation of Works Undertaken

The primary objective of the First Four-Year Plan was to provide Cameroon with vital infrastructure that would stimulate production in all domains. Eighty-five percent of the investment loans of FIDES were dedicated to this goal.[12]

With regard to the road network, the basic program set out to improve existing major roads which provided access to railways and ports, to construct a North-bound axis which would allow improved movement of the products of the Northern region, to eliminate ferries, and to replace temporary bridges with permanent ones, and to reinforce heavily used roads with asphalting.

Consequently, extensive roadwork was undertaken. *Route Razel*, the first section of the Eastbound axis, was opened providing a connection to the industrializing zone of Edéa. Work on the Northbound axis was begun. Its route was to be the following: Bonabéri-Nkongsamba-Foumban-Mayo Darlé-Tibati-Ngaoundéré. It was to allow the opening up of the richest region of the territory and connect with the road to Maroua. Work was begun on the permanent connection between Garoua and Maroua; and on numerous road structures.

The railway system was overhauled. The rolling stock and locomotives worn out by twelve years of intensive use without replacement was gradually renovated; terracing began over the entire line, rails were replaced; and to reduce transportation costs diesel engines replaced the old steam engines. Railway traffic rose from 251,000 tons in 1947 to 554,000 tons in 1951 and to 670,000 tons in 1952.

The building of the Douala-Bonabéri bridge on the Wouri River was certainly the most significant improvement of the export infrastructure of Cameroon. More than 5 billion CFA Francs were devoted to it. The shipping canals of the estuary of the Wouri were deepened. In the port of Douala the construction of seven new wharves was undertaken, as well as terracing for the construction of hangars. The port of Bonabéri, transformed into a banana port, saw the building of a 230-meter wharf. The Bonabéri-Douala link through a dual rail and road bridge over the Wouri River—a project which attracted the special interest of High Commissioner Soucadaux—allowed for the smooth evacuation of the products of the rich western regions. In sum, these projects increased the capacity of the Douala port to an annual traffic of 900,000 tons, and it thus became the third largest port of the West African coast.

Due to the decision to make the economic integration of North Cameroon part of the *mise en valeur* (development) of the territory, the port of Garoua, situated on the Bénoué River, was developed to allow it to handle an annual traffic of 40,000 tons, thus providing access to the products of the northern regions. In the same vein, due to increased production (cocoa, timber) in the hinterland of Kribi, it was decided to extend the harbor installations of the port of Kribi, situated 200 kilometers from Douala. The plans foresaw an annual traffic of 35,000 tons.

In order to complete the long and costly road infrastructure project, beginning in 1950 some airstrips were constructed to allow access to centers lacking permanent roads. It was decided to airlift goods which could not withstand being subjected to long ground transportation. Besides the airport of Douala, the construction of which was financed by the French budget, four other airstrips, Yaoundé, Ngaoundéré, Garoua and Maroua-Salak, were put into service to receive aircraft in all seasons for internal use. They were also

Table 3.3

Changes in the value of exports and imports of Cameroon from 1949 to 1953 (amounts in CFA Francs)

	Exports		Imports	
Year	Total	France	Total	France
1949	6,741	5,201.3	8,775.6	6,378.6
1950	8,190.7	4,747.2	10,561.9	7,246
1951	11,371.9	6,857.1	16,511	11,621.5
1952	11,041.5	5,649.2	18,648.4	11,600.7
1953	13,095.4	5,830.8	14,070.3	8,489.8

Source: "Commerce extérieur du Cameroun oriental, 1946–1966."

supplied with meteorological and radio facilities. At the same time the number of passengers rose from 10,500 in 1950 to 41,500 in 1954 and the amount of merchandise increased from 1,648 to 4,874 tons. Airfields of secondary interest were also built in Foumban, Kribi, and Bertoua. A modern communications network was installed. External links were created to France and French Equatorial Africa. The putting into service of this infrastructure led to considerable development in foreign trade. Table 3.3 shows the growth in the value of exports and imports in Cameroon between 1949 and 1953.

In terms of volume, figures from "*Commerce extérieur du Cameroun oriental*" show that exports increased from 210,259 tons in 1949 to 273,260 tons in 1953. The rise in volume was due much less to an increase in production than to a growth in trade, helped by improvements in communication and lowered transportation costs. The reorganization of *Sociétés Africaines de Prévoyance* and of the packaging of goods, and the education campaigns for producers through films and especially posters, had a positive effect. For example, the care applied in the harvesting, collection and conservation of cocoa and coffee, had as a direct consequence a noticeable improvement in the quality and quantity of exports, especially timber, banana and cocoa.

Between 1949 and 1953 the quantity of imports grew from 211,743 to 288,788 tons. In other words, the index of the volume of imports rose from 47 in 1947 to 153 in 1953, which represents an average annual growth of 35.5 percent. The implementation of the Plan led to considerable growth in imports made possible by the extension of the port of Douala and the general improvement in the means of transportation with the principal centers of the territory. During the 1949–1953 period, the terms of exchange went from an index of 76 in 1948 to 111 in 1953. These numbers attest to the generally positive change in the buying power of producers. Indeed, the price of exported goods grew at a faster rate than that of imported goods.

Internal trade during this period, while continuing to be based on food products, also began to diversify. The shipping of meat by air intensified. While in 1950 it was only 16 tons, it grew to 847 tons by 1953. In 1947, only 10,000 pigs were sold commercially; by 1954, this traffic had grown to 15,000 head. The sale of butter from the factory of Meiganga rose from 37 tons in 1947 to 50 tons in 1952. The local consumption of sea fish, unregulated in 1947, reached 480 tons in 1953 and attained 1,500 tons in 1954. *Brasseries du Cameroun* sold 10,000 hectoliters of beer and *Bastos* sold 10 million packets of cigarettes.

The state effort to develop Cameroonian resources, and the favorable external circumstances of the first years of the Plan were followed by a significant semi-public investment effort encouraged, just as private investments were, by the seeming prosperity of the territory. The French report entitled *"Le Plan et l'évolution du Cameroun"* estimated the total of semi-public investments at 7,500 million CFA Francs for the period 1947–1953. Several semi-public companies were established, among them ENELCAM, an electricity company which was to bring the territory into the industrial phase.

In general, as the report concluded, the end of this period was characterized by euphoria: producers thrived mainly from cocoa, thanks to a favorable international economic climate; traders made investments; the flow of goods was unhindered; the salaried work force found employment thanks to the major work projects undertaken under the impact of the activities of FIDES. However, starting in 1954, unfavorable signs began to appear. In fact, the seeds of decline were already present at the beginning of the 1950s.

The End of the Artificial "Boom"

The "boom" of 1950–1951 was to a great extent artificial and based on speculation; it was not the result of the real but as yet limited growth in production. Marshall Plan payments and especially the implementation of the First Four-Year Plan made possible activities linked to infrastructural equipment, but without corresponding growth in local production, this influx of external loans encouraged inflation. The latter was further aggravated by politically motivated or speculative transfers of capital taking "refuge" in Africa, or attracted by the high profit reaped by public works firms which acknowledged that capital investment could be depreciated in two or three years and still yield a substantial profit margin.

In 1952 a recession began which lasted until 1954. The general situation, as well as the rising budgetary costs caused by the war in Indochina, led to a sharp downturn in FIDES loans. A report by the agency in charge of financial control in Cameroon on trends in public financing in the territory from 1938 to 1953 called attention to "the refusal of the Board of Directors of FIDES to undertake planned activities owing to the general decline in investment loans."[13] As a result, the territory had to abandon several previously planned projects. The reduction of FIDES loans also led to the demise of a number of marginal or opportunistic firms, which had prospered thanks to the bounty of FIDES.

As in the years following the war, the influx of French capital in Africa created uneasiness and imbalance from the beginning of the 1950s on. On this subject it is worth quoting the fifth report presented by the Investment Commission:

> The current situation of the overseas territories is characterized by serious imbalance: indeed the total revenue of overseas territories measured by the value of their production has not noticeably increased since the war, whereas thanks to a policy of economic and social development, the obligations that have been imposed on them and the buying power distributed to certain sectors of the population have greatly increased.

This fundamental imbalance was coupled with a series of secondary imbalances, which were enumerated in the same report:

> Indeed a trade deficit in developing countries is a normal occurrence, but the imbalance has reached disturbing proportions, because the deficit continues to grow even though the proportion of imports of durable goods in relation to the totality of imports is diminishing…
> Imbalance in the distribution of revenues among different categories of the population trigger dangerous migratory movements and lead to the exodus and rush to the rapidly growing urban centers of a floating mass of people who have been released from their traditional social framework and have not been absorbed into the production process.
> Imbalance between the financial resources limited by a rudimentary tax system and budgetary expenses, which are constantly on the rise: these new expenditures, which stem from, among other things, the maintenance and operating of already completed projects in the fields of economic infrastructure, health and educational facilities and the legal system.

Finally, the report called attention to the likely consequences of this situation for France and the entire French Union:

> This situation threatens to force the *métropole* to provide the territories with more assistance. But inasmuch as the latter would serve to make up for the budget deficit, the

portion that could be earmarked for the financing of investments in the French Union would be reduced proportionately.[14]

The same can be said about Cameroon. Although the figures given above for foreign trade convey the economic activity of the territory during the period of the First Four-Year Plan, despite a recovery in 1953, the trade balance deficit did not cease to increase from 1948 to 1953, reaching 5,124.5 million CFA Francs by 1951; in 1953 this deficit was still 974.9 million CFA Francs.[15] In fact, during the entire period, the needs of the territory for durable goods clearly outstripped their production. Imports seemed to have reached a ceiling. As for exports, although they increased steadily, they too reached a peak, starting in 1953.

One of the criticisms made of the First Four-Year Plan in Cameroon was that it had done "almost nothing for black peasants." According to *Cameroun Libre,* which made this observation in its April 15, 1953 edition, billions "have disappeared in spectacular projects. The 'Plan men' (*hommes du Plan*) have no interest whatsoever in the bush. They only see gigantic buildings, oversize hospitals, 12-km wide highways…The bush retains its pitiful dispensaries, its adobe and thatch schools."

This was one of the reasons for the rural exodus of the period. Many Cameroonians took off for the towns, especially Douala, where they found employment thanks to the large-scale projects of the Plan. The population of Douala rose from 51,077 inhabitants in 1947 to 110,000 inhabitants in 1952.[16] This immigration did not affect only Cameroonians. Many Europeans arrived in Cameroon during this period. The white population of the territory rose from 5,800 in 1948 to 13,173 in 1952.[17] This significant influx of Europeans was not appreciated much by Cameroonians; witness the quotation below:

We have no intention of being racist, but we do not wish foreigners to come to enrich themselves in Cameroon, or to monopolize trade without making any investment in the country, occupying positions, which could very well be filled by Cameroonians.[18]

The question of European immigration was raised several times during the meetings of the local assembly. The members of this assembly were not opposed to this immigration as a matter of general principle; they simply demanded that the local administrative authorities make this immigration useful to the territory.[19]

Although many Europeans arriving in Cameroon found employment in construction projects, many others were recruited into the local administration. The year 1951 was a turning point with regard to the size of the public service sector of Cameroon. The growth in the number of civil servants, until then quite steady, suddenly increased sharply. From 1947 to 1950, the overall growth was hardly more than two thousand staff, whereas from 1950 to 1953, it increased to 5,500.[20] The growth was especially important in the sectors in which FIDES made investments. Public opinion considered budget deficits and the growth in the size of the civil service to be inevitable given the magnitude of the effort being made.

There is a correlation between the disbursement of the loans of FIDES and the beginning of the financial difficulties in Cameroon in the early 1950s. It is true that the activities of the *Service du Plan* (the Plan Department) officially began in 1947, the year of the balanced budget in the territory, but on June 30 1949, only 7 percent of the loans of the first plan, representing the first costs of the establishment of firms had been effectively funded.[21] The impact of the first infrastructural projects did not thus begin to be felt on the territorial budget until the 1950 or 1951 fiscal year. At this time, however, for the first time there appeared a budget deficit in the final accounts of the budget. An administrative report gave the following explanation for this deficit:

> Until 1950 the income had always been superior to the expenses, without any significant modifications in the fiscal system other than the adoption of the income tax in 1941.
> The growth in expenditures was not uniform. The personnel and material equipment expenditure rose less quickly than the mandatory expenditures related to subsidies, public works and payments due.
> For a variety of reasons (among which were the inexperience of the financial services, currency devaluation, general measures imposed by France…), the unreliability of budget estimates increased since the war, to the point that the original budgets had to be more or less significantly revised in the course of the fiscal year by further loans which, from 1951 on, were not offset by reliable income.
> This goes a long way to explain budgets, which continuously presented a surplus until 1951; from this year on the balance registered a deficit. After having known a long period of healthy budgets Cameroon began to face serious financial difficulties.[22]

According to the same report, "the excessive size of the projects undertaken in the course of 1951–1952 constituted one of the causes of the indebtedness of the territory and its eventual financial difficulties…"[23] But remarkably, the financial difficulties of the territory seem to have preceded the slowing down of the economic activities which would have explained them. Mostly they had causes which were not economic, but rather purely financial; "these had to do with the circumstances under which the budget had been prepared, voted on and executed, the period of financial euphoria during which they definitely thought themselves richer than they really were."[24]

It is difficult to avoid thinking that the volume of the investments of FIDES must have presented an unbearably heavy burden on the local budget.

In 1953, the French Government itself acknowledged that the consequence of the achievement of the First Four-Year Plan "was indeed a growth in the financial obligations of the territory, not only because of the annual payments to be made to CCFOM, but also owing to the increase in the number of economic and social projects implemented, which automatically entailed a growth in operating and maintenance costs."[25] It was generally accepted that other budgets, and especially the special budget of the Plan, should cover some of the expenditures of the territory. However, the rigidity of the doctrine established by FIDES in this respect made such transfers absolutely necessary. This made *Le Cameroun Libre* denounce the attitude of Paris as follows:

> The situation of French West Africa, French Equatorial Africa, and Cameroon is becoming increasingly more disturbing.
> The reason for this, firstly, is the crushing weight of personnel expenditures. Before the war....these absorbed 30-40 percent of ordinary budgets.
> Today these same personnel expenditures, depending on the territory, take up 60 to 85 percent of ordinary budgets! Accurate computation in some areas shows this number to be as high as 90 percent.[26] One governor, responding to a question about whether he could curtail expenditures in order to avoid imposing new taxes, answered: "How would it be possible when all my expenses go towards paying my staff?"
> This clearly amounts to saying that there is nothing else to do...but put up with the policy imposed by Paris.[27]

For the author of this article, the consequences of this policy were inflation, a fragile and rudderless economy, the closing of firms, and a desperate financial situation. By the beginning of 1953, these consequences became more and more obvious:

> The economy of Cameroon is in bad shape, disturbing noises can be heard about the situation of some firms, investment sources seem to have dried up, construction projects have considerably slowed down, in fact only projects that began in 1952 are being carried out; unemployment rages in the urban centers and we have never seen so many Europeans looking for work, entire families have returned home in the middle of winter under dire circumstances.
> As in French West Africa and French Equatorial Africa, a formidable crisis is threatening, 1953 may lead to a real collapse if the authorities do not take measures to help firms meet their tax and customs obligations, and fight against the constant rise in the cost of living, which will be made even worse by the taxes voted on at the budgetary session of ATCAM.
> If we give in passively to inflation, the current year will witness many more closings, breakups and bankruptcies.
> The goose that lays the golden eggs is in bad shape indeed...
> The artificial prosperity of these last few years was nothing but a facade which is in the course of collapsing...if it continues with its excessive taxation and living "from the blood of colonization" the Administration may no longer find the money to pay itself.[28]

The number of unemployed Europeans in Cameroon did not cease growing, owing to continued layoffs due to cost saving efforts in all firms. Tens of thousands of Africans in urban centers found themselves in the same situation.[29] After the only spinning mill, the most important sawmill of the territory also closed its doors.[30] In 1952 and 1953, several firms were liquidated or went bankrupt.[31] An observer in 1953 noted that things were especially bad in Douala, the economic capital of the territory.

> Despite the influx of people to Douala things are bad, we are told, they are worse and worse. A fancy department store, constructed at great expense on Colonel Leclerc Boulevard, does ridiculously little business: some days their receipts amount to no more than 7,000 francs (CFA)...People come in, look around and don't buy anything. One is forced to think that money is scarce. And yet, in the food stores any price is paid, the ladies pull thousand franc bills out of their handbags as if they were twenties...
>
> Yet, it is undeniable that the crisis is getting worse. The ocean-liners are fully booked until June. No doubt many passengers are only going for vacations, however, many others will not return...
>
> In general, rents in Douala, we are told, have decreased by one third and sometimes by one half. Some people, who had spent fortunes building homes, thinking that the good times will last forever, are now raising their arms to the heavens.
>
> The future, in fact, looks dark for everyone and morale is affected by it.[32]

It is clear that the boom of the early 1950s was ending. Economic activities continued to slow down during the Second Four-Year Plan.

NOTES

1. Oyono (D.), "La politique africaine du Cameroun, 1960–1985," thèse de Doctorat d'Etat, Institut d'Etudes Politiques de Paris, 1988, pp. 51 and following.
2. To this accusation can be added the charge of electoral fraud that Um Nyobè emphasized in his United Nations speeches; see Um Nyobè (R.), pp. 181–186. Morgenthau described in detail the technique used by the French officials to falsify the results of elections in their territories; see Morgenthau (R.S.). *Political Parties in French-Speaking West Africa* (Oxford: the Clarendon Press, 1964). For the particular case of Cameroon, read La *Voix du Cameroun* 15 (May–June 1954), and Mbembe (J.A., ed), *Le problème national Kamerunais* (Paris: L'Harmattan, 1984).
3. See Le Vine (V.T.), *Le Cameroun du mandat à l'indépendance* (Paris: Présence Africaine, 1984), pp. 192–198.
4. See Suret-Canale (J.), p. 81.
5. Chauleur (P.), "Impressions de Dakar," *Marchés Coloniaux*, 275 (February 17, 1951): 459.
6. ANSOM, FIDES 351, "Le Plan et l'évolution du Cameroun 1947–1956," p. 92.

7. *Chroniques d'Outre Mer* (February 1952). In 1953, three important agricultural companies from Indochina, permanently abandoning the Far East, transferred their operations to Cameroon. *Compagnie du Cambodge, Compagnie des Caoutchoucs de Padang* and *Société des Plantations des Terres Rouges* established themselves in the region of Sanaga Maritime, where they had each obtained rural holdings of 1,500 hectares (*Le Cameroun Libre*, 460, December 1953).
8. Durand (H.), *Essai sur la conjoncture de l'Afrique noire* (Paris: Dalloz, 1957), p. 71.
9. Hoffher (R.), *La coopération économique franco-africaine* (Paris: Sirey, 1958), p. 58.
10. "Rapport Annuel du Gouvernement Français" (1952 and 1955).
11. "Les investissements publics nationaux et extérieurs dans les pays francophones d'Afrique tropicale, 1946–1960," Vol. 2, (Paris: IEDES, 1964), p. 50.
12. My account of the projects carried out in Cameroon during the First Plan is based on a variety of French reports, especially "Le Plan et l'évolution du Cameroun" (ANSOM 351. See also Bouchart (P.), "Le FIDES au Cameroun," *Civilisations*, Vol. VI, No. 3, (1956).
13. ANSOM, FIDES 351, "Rapport sur l'évolution des finances publiques au Cameroun entre 1938 et 1953," p. 25.
14. "5ème Rapport de la Commission des investissements," *Statistiques et Etudes financières, supplément finances françaises* 17: 61–62
15. ANSOM, FIDES 351, "Le Plan et l'évolution du Cameroun, 1947–1956," p. 92.
16. Le Vine (V.T.), p. 83.
17. "Notes et Etudes Documentaires. La gestion de la France au Cameroun," p. 24.
18. Cited in *Chroniques d'Outre Mer* (May 1952), p. 43.
19. See *ibid.* pp. 43–44.
20. Richard (R.), "Le budget du Cameroun et les investissements du FIDES," Mémoire de stage, ENA, Paris, (1957), 4.
21. *Ibid.*
22. ANSOM, FIDES 351, "Rapport sur l'évolution des finances publiques au Cameroun," p. 53.
23. *Ibid.* p. 108.
24. *Ibid.* p. 34.
25. "Rapport Annuel du Gouvernement Français" (1953), p. 86.
26. The elevated personnel expenditures were mostly due to the "Lamine Gueye law" and increases in salary payments from 1,512 million CFA in 1950 to 2,468 million in 1951, and then to 3,031 million in 1952. The implementation of the judiciary reform made the annual expenses of the service in question rise from 3 to 124 million between 1945 and 1953 (ANSOM, FIDES 351, "Rapport sur l'évolution des finances publiques," p. 53).
27. *Le Cameroun Libre*, 436 (December 1952): 2.
28. *Le Cameroun Libre*, 439 (15 January 1953): 3.
29. *Ibid.*
30. *L'Eveil du Cameroun*, 438 (January 1, 1953): 1.
31. *Marchés Coloniaux*, 413 (10 October 1953): 2799.
32. "Le ralentissement des affaires à Douala," *Marchés Coloniaux*, 385 (28 March 1953): 986.

Chapter 4

The FIDES Second Four-Year Plan (1953–1956)

The Political Situation in Cameroon

During the Second Four Year Plan relations between the French Administration and the UPC reached a breaking point. This radicalization can be explained by the emergence of new factors, including the events taking place in Indochina and Algeria which no doubt influenced people's attitudes. Three factors influenced the perception of the Cameroon question.

The first factor had to do with French internal politics. From 1946 to 1954 France was engaged in a war with Indochina, a member of the French Union. The defeat at Dien Bien Phu and the Geneva Accords were perceived by the French political and military authorities as a humiliation. Similarly, the outbreak of the war in Algeria in 1954 was considered by France not only to be a challenge to be met, but also a gangrene whose spread had to be immediately stopped. It was essential for the French authorities that the UPC's demands for independence should not create a precedent in Black Africa.

The second factor was related to the international climate. The UPC's demand for independence was unfolding at the height of the Cold War in a zone that was considered to belong to the Western alliance, and the French Administration considered the party to be part of the international communist movement. A few years earlier in Indochina, faced with the attack of the *viet-minh*, France had transformed its colonial war into a sort of crusade to protect the Free World. According to Georges Chaffard, Um Nyobè, Secretary General of the UPC, was considered by his supporters to be the "Cameroonian Hô Chi Minh" at this time.[1]

Finally, to these two factors was added the internal political context. The new High Commissioner, Roland Pré, who arrived in Cameroon in 1954, seemed to be more concerned than his predecessor, André Soucadaux, with the economic development of the territory than with the political debate. This preoccupation, coupled with the question of Indochina and Algeria, made him little inclined to accept the UPC's demand for independence.

The considerable amount of French capital exported since 1946 to Cameroon allowed the launching of intensive infrastructure projects and the growth of the investment of private capital in various firms. But the unfolding of French capitalism in this part of the colonial Empire also created hardships and imbalances, which contributed to and amplified growing discontent in the mid 1950s. The UPC's demands for independence and especially the increasing support for the nationalist movement among a large part of the Cameroonian population seemed to be an expression of this. And "from the moment when the empire becomes one of the elements of French power, all revolutionary ferment provoked by a worsening in the fate of the indigenous population should either be crushed or neutralized by a financial contribution from the *métropole*."[2] In the case of Cameroon the French Government adopted both solutions.

"Financial Contribution": Aims and Capital Investment of the Second Plan

The Capital of the Second Plan: a Compensation for the Withdrawal of Private Capital and a State Duty

Due to the war in Indochina, the French overseas territories were still suffering from restrictions on metropolitan loans in 1954. Paris decided to grant Cameroon a sum of 27.5 billion CFA Francs from 1954 to 1958, as part of the Second Four-Year Plan. This decision was all the more surprising since at that time the words "independence" and "autonomy" were increasingly heard in Cameroon. *Le Cameroun Libre* commented:

> While sometimes a relatively minor project placed on the table of the National Assembly can be discussed in commission, sent back, amended, etc…before finally being voted on, the celestial manna of which Cameroon is going to benefit was acquired through a simple stroke of a magic wand, we are still asking ourselves how, when barely three months ago dismay reigned: it looked as if there was going to be a disastrous reduction in FIDES loans in the 1953–1954 fiscal year…
>
> What happened?
>
> Could it be that the utterance of the word "independence" by the delegation of the "Ngondo" in the cabinet of ministers at the same time as it was before the—very concerned—bodies of the UN, would have had the effect of loosening the purse strings?
>
> The *Commissariat Général du Plan* has suddenly become magnanimous. Its generosity towards Cameroon borders on extravagance, to the point that we are a little worried: won't the other territories be jealous?
>
> Cameroon, adopted child of the French Union, and for some time the most turbulent of

> all on the political level, is so spoilt—at the moment when independence is often talked about—that others could find "fault" with it.[3]

In May 1955, the High Commissioner, Roland Pré, reported social and political activity in Dakar, Brazzaville, and particularly in Cameroon, where it was especially felt, more than elsewhere because Cameroon was a "special territory, a bit like an only son who is especially spoilt." For *Le Cameroun Libre* which commented on this statement all this was paradoxical and worrisome:

> And indeed it is paradoxical. Cameroon is the spoilt child of the French Union. France spends fabulous sums on its equipment and facilities: France's massive public investment intends to make up for the disappearance of private investment. For the latter is scared away by political agitation, social problems, crushing costs directly due to personnel costs which are completely out of proportion with the level of economic development and especially by the continuing promises of emancipation.
> Cameroon is like a spoilt child to whom they always give in.
> In families it usually leads to a bad end.[4]

The above reactions lead to certain statements on the influx of French public capital during the period of the Second Plan. First it can be said that the incoming capital served to ensure public investment, and it indeed compensated for the withdrawal of private capital. This withdrawal began in 1953 and characterized the period from 1953 to 1957, as was highlighted by the French Administration's report on the Plan and the development of Cameroon:

> Although during the period between 1948 and 1953 we have seen a considerable growth in private investment, from 1953 to 1957 we noted an appreciable dip in these investments. Other than the *Société Industrielle des Cacaos* created in 1954, the small firms founded since this time barely deserve mentioning. Some factories even stopped all their activities. In fact the only important investments that were made in the industrial sector were made with semi-public funds. ALUCAM will begin to manufacture alumina in 1957, the oil factory of CFDT will begin producing in 1956, the slaughterhouses of Maroua Salak will be pushed into service starting in 1955. It seems that private capital, discouraged by the generally unfavorable conjuncture that has been in force for three years, is reluctant to invest.[5]

In addition, it can be stated that the exportation of French public capital to Cameroon during the Second Plan was a sovereignty constraint for France. As mentioned earlier, one of the effects of the development of French capitalism was the appearance, from 1951 on, of the phenomenon of budget deficits in the territory. In 1955, the budget deficit of Cameroon reached 1,283,960,534 CFA Francs.[6] This deficit often had to be covered by advances from the French

Treasury, which were to be reimbursed in yearly installments. Thus, Cameroon received a subvention of three billion francs in 1957.[7]

However, the new intervention of French state capitalism also aimed to calm the discontent of the territory's population, the rise of Cameroonian nationalism and ensure the domination of the French colonial state over Cameroonian society through the pursuit of the economic and social development of the territory. It should be recalled that France was accountable to the UN for its activities in Cameroon which she administered for the international body. Therefore France had to avoid all criticism from the international community. In 1952, A. Soucadaux, High Commissioner of Cameroon at the time, anticipated the problem when he declared:

> If despite the difficulties it is undergoing, the *métropole* can continue to grant us the loans necessary for the implementation of the second part of the plan, the prosperity of Cameroon will be one of the best weapons of France in the international debates of tomorrow.[8]

But the new influx of French public capital to Cameroon was an integral part of the new economic orientation decided on early in the 1950s which required new loans.

Loans for European Goals

At the time of its creation the initial goals of FIDES were to "satisfy the needs of the indigenous population" and to "promote the development of the economy of the French Union." But starting in 1951, the main objective of this program was redefined: "to increase agricultural and industrial production with the European community in mind."[9] From this moment on, the colonies were to become increasingly drawn into the French economic system. The old *économie de traite* (trade economy) was replaced by a new *économie d'extraction* (extraction economy).[10] Investments were no longer directed at basic equipment but rather at what was necessary for the extraction or the harvesting of raw materials.

On this question it is interesting to recall some European decisions. The recommendation of the Council of Europe of October 14, 1952 stressed the shortage of raw materials in Europe as well as in the United States, and decided that it was necessary to considerably increase production.[11] Like the Assembly of Strasbourg, the European Organization of Economic Cooperation known as *Organisation Européenne de Coopération Economique* (OECE) emphasized the need to obtain raw materials primarily from overseas countries. The adherence to the principle that raw materials should be purchased at the lowest possible price reinforced the doctrine according to which overseas countries should first and foremost be suppliers of raw materials.

The restrictive texts of the OECE and of the Assembly of Strasbourg regarding the eventual industrialization of the overseas territories further reinforced the view that these two institutions had of this doctrine.[12] The priority was not industrialization but "to increase the export of raw materials towards the *métropole* as well as towards the dollar zone. Thus was imposed the liberal strategy which, this time, assigned to the overseas territories the function of providing the largest possible quantity of raw materials at the lowest possible price."[13] These considerations help to better understand the direction the Second Four-Year Plan took.

It is first necessary to look at the Committee that was charged with the preparation of the Second Plan. Presided over by Governor Roland Pré, this Committee was composed of high-ranking civil servants and representatives of financial and industrial groups which had direct or indirect interests in overseas territories. Among them were: Bernard, industrialist; Brie, CEO of the company in charge of electro-chemistry, electro-metallurgy, and electrical steelworks within the company known as *Ugine*; Gareau Dombasle, CEO of *Compagnie Minière de Conakry*; Gonon, CEO of *Banque de Madagascar*; Lefaucheux, CEO of *Renault*; Lemaigneu, CEO of *Société Commerciale de l'Ouest Africain* (SCOA); de Vitry, CEO of *Péchiney*; and many others. The list of the members of the subcommittees was equally telling: bankers, CEOs of important industrial or commercial companies and semi-public companies, all the representatives of capital had joined forces with the State agents to set the Second Four-Year Plan on its feet.[14]

In the introduction to its report of April 1954, the Committee declared that "the Second Plan intends to carry out the considerable work of substantially raising the living standards of the autochthonous population that had begun in 1946." At the same time, however, the commentary accompanying this declaration of principle leaves one somewhat skeptical:

> The Second Plan, while continuing with investments of a cultural and social nature accords priority to production.
> It would be useless to try to look for long-term solutions (to ensure the substantial raising of the living standards of the autochthonous populations…) without an enormous effort to develop production, which is the basis of any real progress.[15]

As a result, the main goal of the Second Plan for Cameroon was the development of production, namely that of agricultural production

> By the diversification and development of agricultural wealth (hence the creation of breeding farms which will produce well adapted and high yielding species, and the

creation of the modernization sectors which will spread these species to the producers and guide the latter in modern agricultural techniques);
By the intensification of internal trade of the wealth produced (improvement of secondary roads and modernization of the main axes of transportation);
By improving the working conditions of producers (small undertakings of a social character relating to rural engineering, projects of interest to the rural population, water, electricity in the bush which had been much neglected by comparison to urban centers, primary education in rural areas to encourage keeping peasants on their land and to give them a chance of normal development, the provision of preventive medicine to the rural population, etc.);
By educating producers in the sense of giving them a chance to take charge of the various activities which could not be entirely financed by FIDES (partial subventions granted to undertakings of a collective nature, loans for housing and for the producers' associations).[16]

The metropolitan loans granted to Cameroon to encourage the implementation of this program included first those of FIDES which were the most important; the payments made by this organization which are given in detail in table 5.8 (see chapter 5) were 4,268.1 million CFA Francs in 1954, 3,806.9 million in 1955, and 3,501.7 million in 1956. There were also CCFOM loans which were granted to communes, semi-public firms, and private firms. These loans which can be seen in table 5.9 (see chapter 5) amounted to 749.6 million CFA Francs in 1954, 1,453.1 million in 1955, and 1,847.6 million in 1956. Finally, civilian investment for equipment by the state budget shown in table 5.12 (see chapter 5) amounted to 233 million CFA Francs in 1954, 692 million in 1955, and 829 million in 1956.

An analysis of these figures shows that investment made by CCFOM as well as credits from the state budget continued to grow while FIDES loans decreased. The state primarily invested in oil; about 76% of the expenditures of this budget during the period under consideration were dedicated to the exploitation of and prospecting for oil in the territory. CCFOM loans were mostly granted to public-private partnerships and to private firms (about 74% of loans), with the primary goal of temporarily offsetting the effects of private disinvestment which began in 1953.

The withdrawal of private capital explains in part the stagnation, or even relative decrease, of the money supply in Cameroon from 1954 to 1956. According to government figures, the total amount of the means of payment in Cameroon (fiduciary circulation, private credit accounts) went from 11,879 million CFA Francs in 1954 to 11,281 million in 1955, and to 11,208 million in 1956.[17]

Before discussing the impact of the investments of the Second Four Year Plan on the territory, it is important to first look at the costs of local public financing during the same period. What is being considered here include e

Table 4.1

Allocations of the Cameroonian budget for debt service to FIDES from 1954 to 1956 (amounts in CFA Francs)

	1954	1955	1956
Annual repayments of loans	390,740,000	490,339,000	298,453,000
Interest and depreciation of loans	193,771,000	195,298,537	572,400,000
TOTAL	592,511,000	685,638,283	870,853,345

Source: "Cameroun français. Budget"

repayments, such as those of CCFOM loans and advances granted outside FIDES by the local administrations and public companies of Cameroon which are shown in table 5.3 (see chapter 5). According to the figures given in this table, the sums dedicated to these repayments amounted to 78.7 million CFA Francs in 1954, 128 million in 1955, and 185.3 million in 1956. Reimbursements made by local administrations and public companies show a net growth, going from 2.3 million CFA Francs in 1951 to 8.3 million in 1953, to reach 185.3 million in 1956.

The repayments of loans to CCFOM made by the territory have to be added to these repayments. The figures provided by *Institut d'Etude du Développement Economique et Social* (IEDES) show that the latter were more important than the former and their growth was more pronounced, going from 5.4 million CFA Francs in 1952 to 82.1 million in 1954, and to 352.5 million in 1955 to dip to 325 million in 1956.[18]

After 1954, the budgets of Cameroon no longer show the details of the territory's contribution to the functioning of French agencies. Among "expenditures" there is a category for "contributions, subventions, cooperation fund, loans and allocations," which, however, does not indicate the details of the loans. By contrast, the sections pertaining to "public debt" show annual repayments on loans and interests and depreciation of loans and advances granted by the FIDES as summarized in table 4.1.

The Impact of the Second Plan on Cameroon's Economy

The First Four-Year Plan ended in 1953, and with it concluded the phase of large infrastructural projects. The projects undertaken during the Second

Four-Year Plan consisted of the completion or continuation of operations already underway.

At the end of 1956, the following can be said about the territory's infrastructure for economic development.[19] The paved road between Edéa and Douala was completed. The north-bound axis was under construction. Tarring had been completed on the road to the bridge of Nkam. Work was still being undertaken on the Bafang-Bafoussam section. This project was not going to be continued beyond Mayo-Darlé, in part, it was said, for financial reasons (the cost of the project to Ngaoundéré was estimated to be 1,400 million CFA Francs) and in part because of low profitability. The cost of the east-bound axis was lower and would allow the opening up of the Chad region. One part of this project involved a connecting road to French Equatorial Africa. Work was also underway on the Garoua-Maroua route. Besides these major road projects, there were several less significant undertakings. In total, the territory had 12,000 kilometers of roads of which 577 were asphalted and 5,000 were suitable for heavy traffic. Improvement in the main axes of communication followed by the opening up of the richest regions led to considerable growth in the number of automobiles, from 5,074 vehicles in 1949 to 21,531 in 1956.

The bulk of the aviation infrastructure was completed. Besides the airport of Douala, which had been financed by the state budget, and for which a new runway was planned, the four main aerodromes of the territory (Yaoundé, Ngaoundéré, Garoua and Maroua) could be used regularly by the large aircrafts of the period, such as DC4, DC8, and Cargo Nord 2501.

The large project of the development of the Douala port was completed. Projects of lesser importance continued at the port. The Wouri Bridge was opened to traffic in 1955, thus completing the Douala-Bonabéri complex. Further work was planned for the port of Garoua.

The project of modernizing the railways was practically completed; the profitability of investments was over 25 percent. However, the 505 kilometers of railroads remained inadequate and in 1956 the Cameroonian railways company had a deficit of about a 100 million CFA Francs.

The economy of the territory continued to be based on three main export crops: banana, coffee, and especially cocoa. The price of these products, and thus, the income of the producers and the available funds of the territory depended on the market. Speculation, the decline or collapse of the price of these products, as was the case for cocoa in 1956, led to a crisis which caused hardships for the territorial budget, and led to a slowdown of economic activities and hardships for the rural population. The necessity of cushioning these risks as well as of providing the West with agricultural raw materials explains the main direction taken by the Second Four-Year Plan. It stressed the development and diversification of agricultural production. This required a rational organization, which was manifested in the establishment of sectors of agricultural modernization in Cameroon.

These sectors of agricultural modernization were endowed with considerable autonomy. They constituted organizations where producers were associated with the management of local interests and the administrative, financial and technical operation of the organizations involved with the development of production. Each sector was to concentrate its efforts on one or more main crops. There were five sectors: the Cocoa Sector (SEMAC); the sector of high altitude crops (SEMOCAL), which was mostly concerned with the development of coffee and tea growing; the Palm Sector which was established for the production of palm oil; the Eastern Sector (SEMEST) concerned with a variety of crops; and the Northern Sector (SEMNORD) which was entrusted with developing peanut, cotton and rice production and animal husbandry. Cotton growing was the province of a state company known as *Compagnie Française pour le développement des Fibres Textiles* (CFDT). SEMNORD itself was divided into five sub-sectors: the sub-sector of rice-growing at Yagoua; the "herd-book" of Adamaoua charged with the qualitative and quantitative improvement of the cattle stock; the sub-sector of Lara which was entrusted to CFDT; the sub-sector of Guider which was in charge of improving and developing peanut growing; and the sub-sector of Doukoula which was specialized in soil conservation. There were no banana sectors, the production of this crop being under the control of producers' cooperatives.

There were successes in animal husbandry (Wakwa station). Coffee and cotton production increased. But cocoa production stagnated, as did that of peanuts and bananas while palm kernel production decreased. It turned out to be rather difficult to achieve short-term profitability in those operations which tried to improve the agricultural methods of peasants who remained attached to ancestral procedures.

The export figures of the period of the Second Four-Year Plan show this leveling off. Government statistics indicate that exports went from 273,260 tons in 1953 to 310,934 tons in 1955. They also show that there was no increase in value: 13,149.7 million CFA Francs in 1956, as opposed to 13,095.4 million in 1953. It must, however, be mentioned that the value rose to 16,550.5 million in 1955. It was the drop in cocoa prices, and a decrease of 20,000 tons in cocoa and banana production that provoked this decline.

Imports outstripped exports both in tonnage and value. The volume of imports rose from 287,788 tons in 1953 to 350,495 tons in 1956, while their value increased from 14,073.3 million CFA Francs to 16,669.4 million in 1956, after having reached 17,870.9 in 1955.

These indexes of the volume of foreign trade reflect a "pause" in the economy of the territory during the Second Plan. In the case of exports this index is 139 in 1953 and 136 in 1956; for imports it is 153 in 1951 as opposed to 152 in 1956. Despite the decrease in the value of imports, the deficit of the trade balance due to the deteriorating external situation, especially for the price of cocoa, continually worsened after 1954, reaching more than three and a half billion CFA Francs in 1956.

The lowering in the value of exchanges related to this weakened economic situation must also be mentioned. While in 1954, thanks to the increased price of cocoa, the index grew to 148, later on it decreased from 136 in 1955 to 114 in 1956.

Finally, one of the main characteristics of the period of the Second Four-Year Plan was the marked slowdown in private investments. The period also saw the establishment of an agricultural infrastructure directed at developing the totality of Cameroonian resources. However, with few exceptions, efforts in this domain did not yield significant results until 1956. Indeed, since investments were mostly concerned with the establishment of an agricultural infrastructure which would take longer than four years to build, the profitability of agricultural investments would not be evident until after 1957. The deficit in the trade balance increased. A decrease in the imports of certain goods was evident; it was the result of the development of small-scale processing industries.

The importance of capital outflow from France to Cameroon since the beginning of the Plan in 1946 was considerable. However, as J. Marseille remarked, "capital outflow alone does not lead to the solid establishment of the domination of the exporting country."[20] At the end of 1954, the French Government was indeed forced to admit that its policy of the previous six years aimed at trying to slow down the progress of the UPC, the most vigorous element of the nationalist movement in Cameroon, had failed. Despite the difficulties it faced, the UPC advanced throughout the territory while the other competing parties, mostly allied with the local administration, remained stagnant. France's financial contribution did not succeed in neutralizing the revolutionary nationalism of the UPC among Cameroonians. Rather than accepting the UPC's demands for independence, the French Government decided to make a last attempt to silence this radical movement. Given the great popularity of the party and the solidity of its local organizations, this process promised to be long and extremely bloody.

It was in 1955 that the "Cold War" which ravaged the territory at least since 1948 was transformed into actual warfare. In March of that year, violent clashes took place in a number of localities between Cameroonians, many of whom were UPC militants, and forces representing French colonial law. Then in May, riots occurred in several towns of southern Cameroon. Many people were killed and others wounded.[21]

Both the Administration and the UPC mutually accused each other of being responsible for the riots. However, the incidents of May provided the colonial authorities with an excuse for dismantling and destroying the UPC. While the Administration was attempting to eliminate the UPC in Cameroon, efforts were also being made in Paris to legally ban this party from Cameroonian political life. On July 2, 1955, at the meeting organized in Conakry, Guinea, by the *Comité de Coordination* of the *Rassemblement Démocratique Africain* (RDA), the UPC as well as two other radical sections of the RDA, the *Union Démocratique Sénégalaise* and the *Parti Progressiste Nigérien*, were expelled from the RDA. It must be recalled that the UPC had steadfastly refused to follow the strategy of Houphouët Boigny, leader of the RDA who, after 1950, broke ties with the French Communist Party. However, the main reason that led to the expulsion of the UPC from the RDA in 1955 is the same as that which motivated the French Government's repression, that is the hostility to an organization which refused to give up its demand for the independence of Cameroon in favor of integration into the French Union.[22]

It was also for the same reason that on July 13, 1955 the French Government presided over by Edgar Faure, who had recently replaced Pierre Mendès-France, banned the UPC as well as its subsidiary youth and women's organizations, *Jeunesse Démocratique Camerounaise* (JDC), and *Union Démocratique des Femmes Camerounaises* (UDFC). From that time on, armed struggle became the only choice for the UPC. The party was forced into a bloody conflict which began in December 1956 and was to last for several years.

NOTES

1. Chaffard (G.), *Les carnets secrets de la décolonisation*, vol. 1 et 2 (Paris: Calman Levy, 1967), p. 361.
2. Marseille (J.), *Empire colonial et capitalisme français. Histoire d'un divorce* (Paris: Albin Michel, 1984), pp. 151–152.
3. *Le Cameroun Libre*, 474 (July 1–15, 1954): 1.
4. "La ruine de l'économie du Cameroun stopperait la progression sociale," *Le Cameroun Libre*, 495 (May 15–31): 1.
5. ANSOM, FIDES 351, "Le Plan et l'évolution du Cameroun 1947–1956," p. 96.
6. "Deux milliards de subvention pour le Cameroun," *La Presse du Cameroun* (November 14). The deficit was 780 million in 1951, 551 million in 1952 (ANSOM, FIDES 351, "Rapport sur l'évolution des finances publiques," p. 31).
7. Grassard (J.), "Le budget du Cameroun pour 1955," *La Nouvelle Revue de la France d'Outre Mer*, 2 (February 1952): 49–50.
8. Cited in *Chronique d'Outre mer* (February 1952): 49–50.

9. Davidson (B.), *L'Afrique au XXè siècle* (Paris: Jeune Afrique, 1979), p. 210.
10. See *ibid* and Marseille (J.), p. 273.
11. See *Le Cameroun Libre*, 438 (January 1, 1953): 1–4.
12. See *Marchés Coloniaux*, 414 (October 17, 1953): 2821–2823.
13. Marseille (J.), p. 275.
14. Dumaine (A.L.), "La signification réelle du second plan," *Présence Africaine* (April–July 1955): 67.
15. Cited by Dumaine, *Ibid.*
16. "Rapport Annuel du Gouvernement Français" (1957), p. 108.
17. "Rapport Annuel du Gouvernement Français" (1956), p. 310.
18. "Les investissements publics nationaux," p. 50.
19. The following presentation is based on various archival documents the most important among which are the report entitled "Le Plan et l'évolution du Cameroun, 1947–1956" (ANSOM, FIDES 351, pp. 93 and following) and data from "Commerce extérieur du Cameroun oriental."
20. Marseille (J.), p. 150.
21. The colonial administration presented the following assessment of the riots of May 1955: 1 dead and 62 wounded among the forces of order; 4 dead (2 Africans and 2 Europeans) and 13 wounded (11 Europeans and 2 Africans) among the civilian population; 20 dead and 114 wounded among the demonstrators; 357 arrested and 85 warrants issued. For a summary of these riots, see: Atangana (M.), *Capitalisme et nationalisme au Cameroun au lendemain de la Seconde Guerre Mondiale, 1946–1956* (Paris: Publications de la Sorbonne, 1998), pp. 157–159; "Cameroun 1955. Les Emeutes de mai" (Service de l'information); and "Emeutes sanglantes au Cameroun" (*Marchés Coloniaux*, June 4, 1955, p. 1509).
22. See *Inter-Afrique Presse* (June 2, 1955): 12.

Chapter 5

Financial Assessments of Public Investment

There are many statistical sources on public capital invested in Cameroon from 1946 to 1956. The figures vary according to the sources, but not all of these sources are reliable. The assessment that will be made in this chapter is for the most part based on data from the excellent study, already cited several times, conducted by IEDES researchers, who used the figures provided by CCFOM which was the principal instrument of the mobilization of French overseas public investment during the period of this study.[1] From 1947 to 1959, the CCFOM issued its financial position, monthly or annually. I have had the opportunity to consult these CCFOM documents for the purpose of comparing and cross-checking data. The CCFOM documents can be found in the French Overseas Archives at Aix-en-Provence, France.

Assessments made here concern investment realized in the public sector with capital of local and metropolitan origin, private investment made with medium term credit, the set up of companies and capital increases, and intangible research expenditures. The available financial information on the types of investments was to some extent statistically centralized. This centralization, however, is lacking with regard to long-term private borrowing and self-financing of modern firms.

Finally, it should be noted that the assessments are in CFA Francs after conversion from French francs. To recall, one CFA franc during the period of this study was worth 1.70 French francs in 1946 and 1947, 1.76 French francs in 1948, and 2 French francs during the rest of the period.

The Final Cost of Internal Public Financing

The necessity of assessing the investments made in Cameroon from the local budget has already been underlined: such assessments make it possible to measure the amount of metropolitan capital which was exported to Cameroon, to quantify French economic intervention in the territory, and to assess the ability of the colonial state to impose its views and authority. The calculation of the final costs of the internal public financing consists of evaluating, aside from the public investments of local funds or "gross investments," the various financial flows whose purpose was to increase the volume of French investment in Cameroon. These financial flows were primarily the result of the following operations: repayments by the territory of advances that had been granted to it by CCFOM within the framework of FIDES; repayments by public organizations (urban and rural communes, ports, railways, Chamber of Commerce, etc.), of loans and advances granted by CCFOM outside of FIDES; and Cameroon's own participation in the FIDES program.

Information about these movements can be supplemented from the year-end financial statements of CCFOM and FIDES of December 31. These statements make it possible to differentiate between the payments disbursed, on the one hand, and the redemption of loans, on the other. The interest paid by the recipients of these loans is not taken into consideration. In the budget of the territory, already presented in the preceding chapters, the interest figures and depreciation payments appeared in consolidated form, as did the figures of the loan annuities and the contributions of the territory to the functioning of certain French services. But an assessment of the flood of capital from Cameroon to France, based on these figures will be misleading, inasmuch as the budgets consulted only are comprised of entries which do not correspond to the actual amounts paid. Thus assessments made here will be based only on the "financial statements" of FIDES and CCFOM. However, the amounts of payment orders relating to the contribution of Cameroon to French services will be included; it should be mentioned that the schedules which could be recovered from archival documents, only cover the period from 1946 to 1950.

The following tables recapitulate the final cost of internal public investment: table 5.1 indicates gross investment from internal financing; table 5.2 is on Cameroon's own contribution to FIDES and repayments by the territory of loans and advances from CCFOM under FIDES; table 5.3 details the repayments of loans and advances, above and beyond FIDES, of CCFOM by local public organizations and companies; table 5.4 shows the investments of the Cameroonian budget from local funds; table 5.5 is dedicated to payment orders from the local budget for the contribution of the territory to the functioning of French services such as *Caisse Intercoloniale des Retraites, Bureau International de Berne*, postal services and organizations, *Ecole Africaine de Médecine et de Pharmacie de Dakar*; *Service Géographique*, *Institut International Seymour*, *Institut de Météorologie*, organizations and publications of scientific and cultural interest, *Bureau d'Accueil d'Alger*, *Centre Acridien du Soudan*, and *Centre des Hautes Etudes Musulmanes*; and table 5.6 shows the final costs of internal public financing.

Table 5.1

Gross capital investment from internal financing from 1946 to 1956 (amounts in millions of CFA Francs)

	1946	1947	1948	1949	1950
Budget	101.3	87.3	377.8	599.3	884.7
Railways	21.0	14.0	26.5	33.0	38.0
Port budget	2.0				
Cocoa account				82.0	196.0
Communal budgets	5.2	11.2	18.5	30.0	42.8
TOTAL	129.5	112.5	422.8	744.4	1,161.5

	1951	1952	1953	1954	1955	1956
Budget	883.8	2,053.4	1,516.2	580.8	1,143.2	421.1
Railways	182.0	33.8	233.8	278.0	399.8	138.8
Port budget		161.1	260.0	300.0	351.2	136.9
Cocoa account	324.5	605.0	219.0			
Communal budgets	68.0	89.5	111.2	101.1	111.4	113.9
TOTAL	1,458.3	2,942.8	2,340.2	1,259,9	1,985.6	810.8

Source: adapted from "Les investissements publics nationaux" vol II, p. 45.

Table 5.2

Cameroon's own contribution to FIDES and repayments of CCFOM loans under FIDES from 1946 to 1956 (amounts in million of CFA Francs)

	1946–51	1952	1953	1954	1955	1956
Contributions						
Repayments		5.4		82.1	352.5	325.0
TOTAL		5.4		82.1	352.5	325.0

Source: adapted from "Les investissements publics nationaux" vol II, p. 50.

Table 5.3

Repayments of non-FIDES loans from CCFOM by local public organizations and companies from 1946 to 1956 (amounts in million of CFA Francs)

	1946–50	1951	1952	1953	1954	1955	1956
Local budget		2.0	4.2	4.2	61.2	78.5	111.3
Communes		0.3	2.1	4.4	16.6	20.3	19.0
Other organizations							47.5
Public companies					0.9	29.2	7.5
TOTAL		2.3	6.3	8.6	78.7	128	185.3

Source: adapted from "Les investissements publics nationaux" vol II, p. 55.

Table 5.4

Investments of the Cameroonian budget from local funds from 1946 to 1956 (amounts in million of CFA Francs)

	Infra-Structures	New buildings	Acquisition of materials	Transfers	TOTAL
1946	24.2	22.3	54.8		101.3
1947	13.7	6.6	67.0		87.3
1948	43.9	130.6	87.4	115.9	377.8
1949	66.8	285.4	193.4	53.7	599.3
1950	162.4	432.4	287.4	2.5	884.7
1951	66.0	659.6	158.2		883.8
1952	81.8	1,780.2	191.4		2,053.4
1953	509.4	679.0	283.8	44.0	1,516.2
1954	210.8	103.8	266.2		580.8
1955	412.0	273.0	417.2	41.0	1,143.2
1956	111.9	72.5	234.4	2.4	421.2

Source: adapted from "Les investissements publics nationaux" vol II, p. 17.

Table 5.5

Payment orders of the Cameroonian budget for contributions to the functioning of French services and organizations, from 1946 to 1950 (amounts in CFA Francs)

	1946	1947	1948	1949	1950
A	205,946.5	918,838	2,171,150	567,460	
B	17,388				
C				9,882.5	429,030
D		1,014,000			
E				7,450,000	10,190,000
F	10,764.7				
G	20,000				
H	26,356				
I		754,000			
J				7,500,000	7,500,000
K			22,740		51,697
L					54,558
M				29,800	
N				150,000	
O					2,717,875
P					100,000
Q					310,480.5
T	280,455.2	2,686,833	2,193,890	15,707,142	21,353,540,5

Source: ANSOM, affaires économiques 84. This source does not specify whether the figures are adjusted for inflation or not.

A: *Caisse Intercoloniale des Retraites.*
B: *Bureau International de Berne.*
C: Postal services and organizations.
D: *Ecole de Médecine et de Pharmacie de Dakar.*
E: *Service Géographique.*
F: Treasury expenses.
G: *Institut International Seymour.*
H: Accountancy expenses.
I: Contribution to colleges.
J: War damages.
K: *Institut de Meteorology.*
L: Organizations and publications of scientific and cultural interest.

M: *Bureau d'Accueil d'Alger.*
N: Organizing of the show of colonial engineers.
O: *Centre Acridien du Soudan.*
P: *Centre des Hautes Etudes Musulmanes.*
Q: Expenses for the delegation of Cameroon.
T: TOTAL.

Table 5.6

Final cost of internal public financing or French investments from Cameroonian funds from 1946 to 1956 (amounts in millions of CFA Francs)

YEAR	AMOUNT
1946	129.5
1947	112.5
1948	422.8
1949	744.3
1950	1,161.5
1951	1,460.6
1952	2,954.5
1953	2,348.8
1954	1,420.7
1955	2,466.1
1956	1,321.1

Source: adapted from "Les investissements publics nationaux" vol II, p. 57.

Public Capital of Metropolitan Origin

Metropolitan public capital invested in Cameroon had three sources: FIDES, CCFOM, and the French state budget. The investment activities taken from these sources sometimes appear in the form of transfers and grants, loans, advances and contributions, sometimes in direct spending.

Loan transactions were mostly carried out by CCFOM, which acted as a public banking institution. The French State contributed to the financing of investments either by direct spending, or by contributions to semi-public companies, or by equipment grants to the local budget. Created by Article 3 of the Law of April 30, 1946, FIDES was to provide financing for the development plans in Cameroon as well as in the other territories under French rule.

having provided nearly one quarter of the total. With a little more than 16 percent of the total investments, the capital of CCFOM only comes in third place. Finally, the contribution of the French national budget was very low, since it constituted about only 4 percent of the total capital investment.

Secondly, it can be stated that after a net growth in investments from 1947 to 1952, there was a decrease from 1953 on, that is to say from about the time of the end of the First Four-Year Plan and the beginning of the Second Plan. The sums expended during the First Plan were almost double those spent during the Second Plan. For economic and strategic reasons, the French attributed special importance to infrastructure in Cameroon after the end of the war. More than 70 percent of FIDES total loans were invested in this sector from 1946 to 1956. For the period of the First Four-Year Plan alone, this was 86 percent. The subsequent drop in investments during the Second Plan can be understood in light of the fact that the bulk of the infrastructural projects had been undertaken during the First Plan.

Table 5.7

Civilian capital spending in the French national budget for Cameroon from 1946 to 1956 (amounts in millions of CFA Francs)

	Aviation Infrastructure	Other direct budgetary spending (a)	Contributions of BRP to SEREPCA (b)	TOTAL
1946	7			7
1947	8			8
1948	32			32
1949	10			10
1950	3		13	16
1951	28		75	103
1952	120		77	197
1953	105	30	135	270
1954	13		220	233
1955	140		552	692
1956	175	81	573	829

Source: adapted from "Les investissements publics nationaux" vol II, p. 92.

(a) All other investments financed by the French budget are listed under this category.

(b) BRP: *Bureau des Recherches Pétrolières*; SEREPCA: *Société d'Exploitation et des Recherches Pétrolières au Cameroun.*

Figure 5.1

French public investment in Cameroon from 1946 to 1956

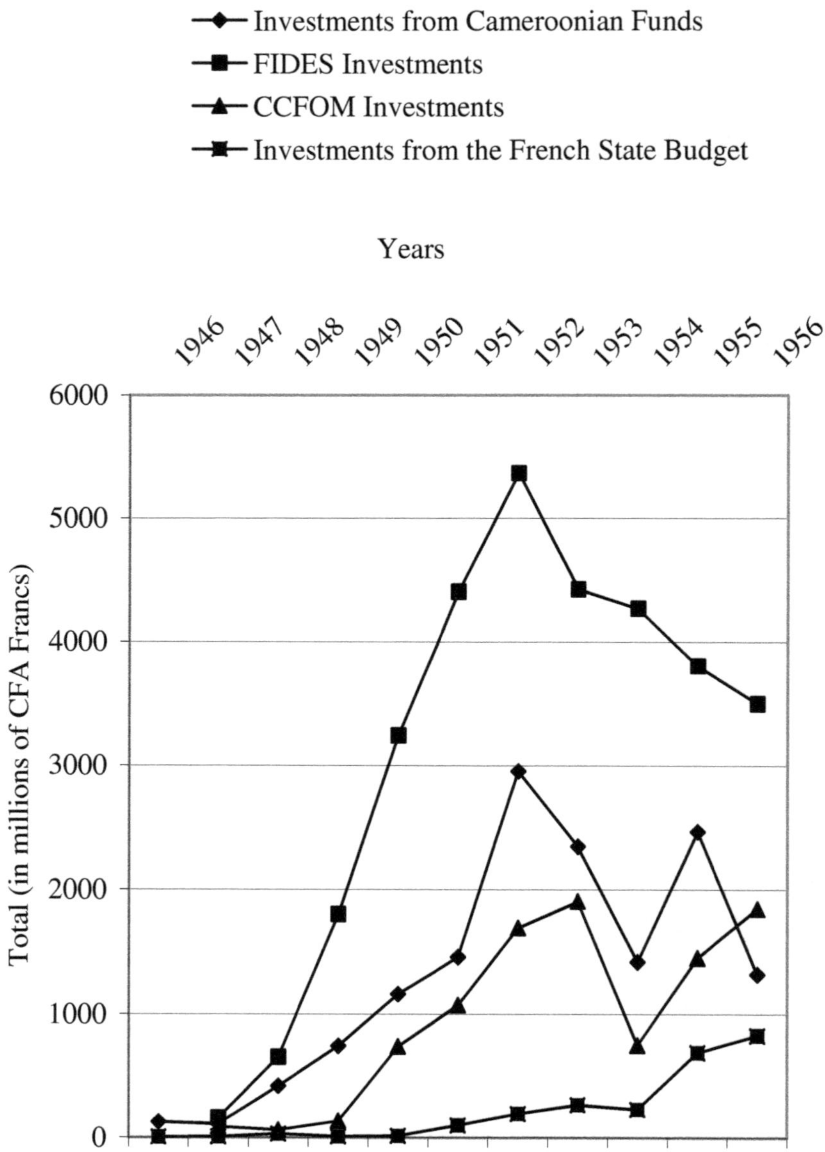

Table 5.8

Payments made by FIDES from 1946 to 1956 (amounts in millions of CFA Francs)

	1947	1948	1949	1950	1951
GENERAL SECTION	9.1	28.3	212.7	404.3	531
LOCAL SECTION 1st Plan : General spending	1.6	6.5	16.5	29.5	40.2
Production	16.2	66.3	168.1	300.1	409.3
Transportation and communication	120.4	493.6	1,251.7	2,234.2	3,046.9
Social infrastructure	14.7	60.3	152.9	272.9	372.2
TOTAL 1st Plan	152.9	626.7	1,589.2	2,836.7	3,868.6
TOTAL	162.0	655.0	1,801.9	3,241.1	4,399.8

	1952	1953	1954	1955	1956
GENERAL SECTION	240.1	266.7	223.0	787.0	287.0
LOCAL SECTION 1st Plan : General spending	53.3	32.6	9.6		
Production	542.2	331.6	97.8		
Transportation and communication	4,035.9	2,468.4	728.1		
Social infrastructure	493.0	301.5	88.9		
TOTAL 1st Plan	512.4	3,134.1	924.4		
2nd Plan : General spending					
Production		404.6	1,238.9	1,198.9	1,276.2
Transportation and communication		415.8	1,273.3	1,232.1	1,311.6
Social infrastructure		198.7	608.5	588.9	626.9
TOTAL 2nd Plan		1,019.1	3,120.7	3,019.9	3,214.7
TOTAL	5,364.5	4,419.9	4,268.1	3,806,9	3,501.7

Source: adapted from "Les investissements publics nationaux" vol II, p. 78.

Table 5.9

CCFOM investments from 1946 to 1956 (in millions of CFA Francs)

	Territory	Communes	Semi public companies	Private companies	TOTAL
1947				80.5	80.5
1948				64.0	64.0
1949	20.2		52.0	63.4	135.6
1950		15.0	428.0	297.5	740.5
1951	100.0	85.0	706.7	179.9	1,071.6
1952	83.0	25.0	1,371.1	215.3	1,694.4
1953	629.0	140.0	954.4	183.8	1,907.2
1954	454.7	94.0	80.0	120.9	749.6
1955	115.0	117.0	714.3	506.8	1,453.1
1956	225.0	50.0	672.6	900.0	1,847.6

Source: adapted from "Les investissements publics nationaux" vol II, p. 88.

Table 5.10

Investment in Black Africa from local public funds (in millions of CFA Francs)

	Cameroon	FEA	Togo	Mada-gascar	FWA	TOTAL
1946	129.5	446.4	43.6	281.7	964.6	1,865.8
1947	112.5	535.2	52.5	583.4	1,069.9	2,353.5
1948	422.8	503.2	58.3	807.4	2,465.6	4,256.3
1949	744.3	1,168.8	120.3	1,288.8	4,114.1	7,436.3
1950	1,161.5	1,461.6	137.6	1,586.5	6,211.3	10,558.5
1951	1,458.3	1,670.7	189.4	1,842.0	8,195.6	13,356.0
1952	2,942.8	2,229.7	314.2	3,316.1	10,882.0	19,684.8
1953	2,340.2	1,567.6	210.5	3,413.5	11,086.2	18,618.0
1954	1,259.9	1,096.8	208.3	3,623.5	11,886.2	18,075.3
1955	1,985.6	977.4	228.4	3,793.1	12,453.4	19,437.9
1956	810.8	1,065.5	184.6	3,672.8	11,221.4	16,955.1

Source: adapted from "Les investissements publics nationaux" vol II.

Table 5.13

FIDES investments in Black Africa, from 1947 to 1956 (amounts in millions of CFA Francs)

	1947	1948	1949	1950	1951
Cameroon	162.0	655.0	1,801.9	3,241.1	4,399.8
FWA	1,922.6	3,555.9	6,672.1	6,263.1	8,126.3
Togo	20.4	20.4	439.7	432.9	284.3
FEA	80.0	361.6	1,855.5	4,388.6	4,849.9
Madagascar	110.9	681.3	1,557.6	2,189.0	2,775.0
Shared expenditures, not broken-down	485.2	813.8	1,781.5	1,826.9	1,745.1
TOTAL	2,781.1	6,131.6	14,108.3	18,341.6	22,179.4

	1952	1953	1954	1955	1956
Cameroon	5,364.5	4,419.9	4,268.1	3,806.9	3,501.7
FWA	23,273.3	11,947.4	10,350.0	9,159.2	12,720.6
Togo	706.1	374.8	463.2	395.6	520.4
FEA	4,341.4	4,103.4	5,278.6	5,606.1	5,429.5
Madagascar	4,623.3	3,087.4	3,083.8	3,200.2	3 ,437.6
Shared expenditures, not broken-down	1,428.6	1,475.3	1,773.7	1,928.1	2,233.9
TOTAL	39,737.2	25,408.2	25,218.3	24,096.1	27,843.7

Source: adapted from "Les investissements publics nationaux" vol II.

The figures from the above tables suggest the following observations about French public investment in Black Africa from 1946 to 1956. Concerning investment from local sources, from a total of 132,597.5 million CFA Francs, the contribution of the Cameroonian budget was 13,368.2 million, that is to say about 10 percent of the total. As for the FIDES investments, from a total of 205,844.5 million CFA Francs, the territory received 31,620.9 million, that is to say about 15 percent of the total. These figures put Cameroon almost on a par with French Equatorial Africa (34,438.1; 16,7 percent), and ahead of Madagascar (24,746.1; 12,02 percent), and Togo (3,701.4; 1.7 percent). Cameroon's contribution is even more striking in the case of investments made from the CCFOM financing: 9,743.6

Table 5.14

Distribution by territory of the FIDES and CCFOM credits until the end of 1955 (amounts in billions of French francs)

	FIDES (local section)	FIDES (overseas section)	CCFOM (non FIDES Investment)	TOTAL	Percent-age
FWA	12.5	168.1	26.4	207	38
FEA	6.7	62.5	27	96.2	18
Cameroon	4.3	53.9	32	90.1	17
Togo		7.1	0.3	7.4	1.4
Madagascar & Comoros	3.7	49.3	13.8	67.4	12.5
Pacific Islands	1.7	9.8	7	18.5	3.1
Saint Pierre		1.4	0.1	1.5	0.3
Somalis		6.2	0.1	6.3	1.3
General spending	44.2		2.3	46.5	8.4
TOTAL	73	358.9	109	540.9	100

Source: Atangana (M), "French Capitalism and Nationalism in Cameroon", p. 92.

million CFA Francs, from a total of 32,465.5 million, or approximately 30 percent of these investments. By contrast, Cameroon's share in the budgetary spending of the French State is meager. This budget allocated 2,397 million to Cameroon, that is to say 7.7 percent of the total spending which amounted to 31,023 million.

When computing public investments made in Black Africa from 1946 to 1957 from metropolitan funds, it appears that from a total of 269,334 million CFA Francs 43,761.5 million (about 16 percent of the total) went to Cameroon.

An analysis of the overall French investment in overseas territories shows that Cameroon's role was also significant. Table 5.14 and figure 5.2, concerning the distribution of overseas investments by FIDES and CCFOM since their inception until 1955, show well the place of Cameroon in French overseas public investment. It appears that since the launching of the public equipment program for the overseas territories financed by FIDES in 1946, the

Table 2.3

Payment of annuities, interest and loan payments, and contributions of Cameroon to the functioning of French organizations and services from 1946 to 1949 (amounts in CFA Francs)

	1946	1947	1948	1949
Annual repayment of loans	2,612,590	2,630,000	2,496,690	2,621,540
Interest and amortization of loans		5,000,000	8,398,931	88,550,000
Contributions of the territory	8,086,000	9,868,000	6,400,000	21,021,000
TOTAL	10,698,590	17,498,000	17,295,621	112,192,540

Source: "Cameroun Français. Budget."

The other "contributions of the territory" were constituted by payments related to war reparations made by the French Union as a whole, the payments of aid in France, subventions to the *Touring-Club* of France, etc. In the Cameroonian budget the credits for these expenses are noted in the chapters reserved for "payable debt." Table 2.3 shows these loans from 1946 to 1949.

The study of the movements of capital would be incomplete without an assessment of private capital. This question will be dealt with later in chapters 6 and 7.

The transfer of capital between France and Cameroon was facilitated by the existence of the "franc zone" which was created in 1945. This was a monetary union between the French colonies of Africa, the Pacific region and Indochina. The system envisioned the free convertibility of currencies at a fixed rate. It also envisioned a unification of accounts. The French Treasury was intended to centralize the resources of the treasuries of the overseas countries and to meet their financial needs. The foreign exchange offices were thus to obey the orders of the Foreign Exchange Office of Paris, and all currencies were centralized in Paris. The management of the overseas exchange offices was entrusted to CCFOM. The Exchange Bureau of Cameroon was thus receiving its instructions from CCFOM. P. Hugon discussed the advantages and drawbacks of the franc zone for Cameroon when he wrote that

The loans shown above went to the public sector such as the Department of Public Works, *Régie des Chemins de Fer* (the railway company), and *Institut des Huiles et Oléagineux Tropicaux* (IRHO—Institute for Oil and Oleaginous Plants), as well as to the private sector including forestry companies, public works firms, and various industries. The distribution of the loans, especially those allocated to Cameroon for the first phase of the Marshall Plan, was the object of a protest in December 1948 by ARCAM, which believed that this distribution "was made arbitrarily to the advantage of three exclusive beneficiaries without taking into consideration the proposals made by the local government to address forestry, agricultural, mining and industrial needs."[24]

Before turning to the consequences of the influx of capital from France, it is interesting to look at the capital flow in the opposite direction, that is to say from Cameroon to France. Until 1950 there had been no reimbursement of the non-FIDES loans and advances of CCFOM by local public organizations and firms. At the same time, during the entire decade of 1946–1956 there was no contribution on behalf of the territory to FIDES, and there was no reimbursement of the loans and advances which were granted by CCFOM as part of the FIDES program until 1951. The budgets of Cameroon give not only the amounts that the territory dedicated to the annual repayments of loans, but also to the interest payments and repayment of loans authorized by FIDES. The territory also contributed to the functioning of numerous French services a list of which follows:

Recherche Scientifique Coloniale
Chaires d'Enseignements Coloniaux
Caisse Intercoloniale des Retraites
Ecole Nationale de la France d'Outre Mer
Contrôle financier des compagnies de chemin de fer relevant du Ministère des Colonies
Bureau International de Berne
Agence Comptable des Timbre Poste Coloniaux
Ecole Africaine de Médicine et de Pharmacie de Dakar
Service Géographique de l'AEF-Cameroun
Laboratoire du Service Vétérinaire de Fort Lamy
Service Intercolonial d'Information et de Documentation
Ecole Nationale des Eaux et Forêts de Nancy
Service Social Colonial
Conseil National des Assurances
Institut Météorologique International
Ecole William Ponty de Rufisque
Various organizations and publications of scientific and cultural interest

From a legal point of view, FIDES was a single account among the entries of CCFOM which exercised the rights and fulfilled the functions that had been assigned to it by the Decree of February 2, 1944 and by the Law of April 30, 1946 related to the establishment, financing, and implementation of development plans for the territories under the purview of France Overseas Ministry.

It must be recalled that the resources of FIDES were of two kinds: a subsidy determined every year by the Finance Law; the contributions of the territory either from its own resources or—this was generally the case—from long term advances that the CCFOM granted based on the anticipated needs for the implementation of the approved programs.

FIDES operations were divided into two sections: first a general section that was fully financed by the French Treasury and provided support for shared expenditures, including studies, scientific and mining research, as well as State acquisitions in the major energy and mining concerns; secondly an overseas section supported by the contribution of the territories from the advances of CCFOM and from a subsidy by the French State, which financed local projects and activities.

The general principle for an assessment of investments made by FIDES is to examine the investment at the level of actual spending as expressed by payments made. Such an assessment can be made based on the "financial statement of CCFOM," drawn on June 30 of each year, from 1947 to 1959.

CCFOM was the main instrument for mobilizing French public investments in Cameroon. Assessments made here only take into consideration the organization's own transactions, that is to say its transactions outside of FIDES, carried out in keeping with the Law of April 30, 1946, to help finance programs foreseen by the Plan.

Thus, the assessment of CCFOM investment made here will exclude: medium term rediscount transactions; granting of endorsement backing for the financing of procurement contracts; and CCFOM advances whose duration and goals make them pure cash advances. CCFOM operations considered here are those which contributed to gross capital formation. They concern firstly loans and advances granted to the territory, to local public organizations (communes, chambers of commerce, the national railway company, etc), to firms with public financing (energy companies, real estate companies), and to private firms; and secondly contributions to the capital of semi-public companies, state-owned companies, and private firms. The financial statements of CCFOM on December 31 of each year (from 1947 to 1959) make such an assessment possible.

The French national budget contributed to the spending for equipment made by various French ministries, such as the Ministry of Overseas France and the Ministry of Public Works. In addition, many FIDES and CCFOM investment projects received subsidies or grants from the French budget.

The operating expenses related to scientific research will also be considered here. These expenses were for the most part dedicated to the remuneration of researchers. They were the responsibility of certain organizations or institutions with a special status which were funded entirely or in part from metropolitan budgets (*Office de la Recherche Scientifique et Technique d'Outre Mer [ORSTOM]*, *Commissariat à l'Energie Atomique*, research institutes, etc). There is also the case of the expenses of oil exploration research attached to the *Bureau de Recherches Pétrolières* (BRP). This institution received the quasi-totality of its funding from the State. What characterized these investments was the general interest they served (aeronautics, maritime signaling) and the complexity of their allocations (*ORSTOM, Energie Atomique, Bureau Minier*, etc.)

Military spending is excluded from the assessments made in this study. The main reason for this exclusion is that "the variety of financing methods, the multiplicity of services and organizations, even the distribution of loans among the different budgets make it very difficult to determine (or even to assess) the State's budgetary spending in the former overseas territories."[2] Also, responding to strategic imperatives, these expenses in general had little impact or influence on Cameroonian society.

Finally, regarding the actual Marshall aid earmarked for the development of the overseas territories, the exchange value in francs passed through CCFOM. Therefore, this aid will be noted into the accounts at the same time as the running operations of the organization under FIDES (CCFOM advances for participation in FIDES). It is important to realize that the Marshall Plan for the overseas territories was kept separate only in reference to the allocation of currencies. In Cameroon, as elsewhere in Africa, the Marshall Plan played an important role by facilitating the reconstruction of the heavy equipment stock necessary for the major infrastructural works to be carried out in the territory.

The following tables summarize the assessment of public capital invested in Cameroon from 1946 to 1956 by the French national budget (table 5.7), FIDES (table 5.8), and CCFOM (table 5.9). To these tables will be added figure 5.1 which makes it easier to have a quick overview of the development of French public investment in Cameroon and the relative importance of each source of financing.

An examination of these tables and figure leads to certain observations. Firstly, the funds deriving from FIDES were the most important; actually they constituted more than half (approximately 54 percent) of the total capital invested by France in Cameroon from 1946 to 1956. It is interesting to note that the Cameroonian budget was the second largest source of investment,

Table 5.12

Cameroon's contribution to non military spending in the French national budget for Black Africa from 1946 to 1956 (amounts in millions of CFA Francs)

	Cameroon	From an overall total of
1946	7	779
1947	8	1,231
1948	32	2,402
1949	10	3,024
1950	16	2,849
1951	103	2,688
1952	197	3,060
1953	270	3,274
1954	233	3,097
1955	692	3,638
1956	829	4,981

Source: adapted from "Les investissements publics nationaux" vol II, p. 92.

Figure 5.2

Distribution by territory of the FIDES and CCFOM loans until the end of 1955

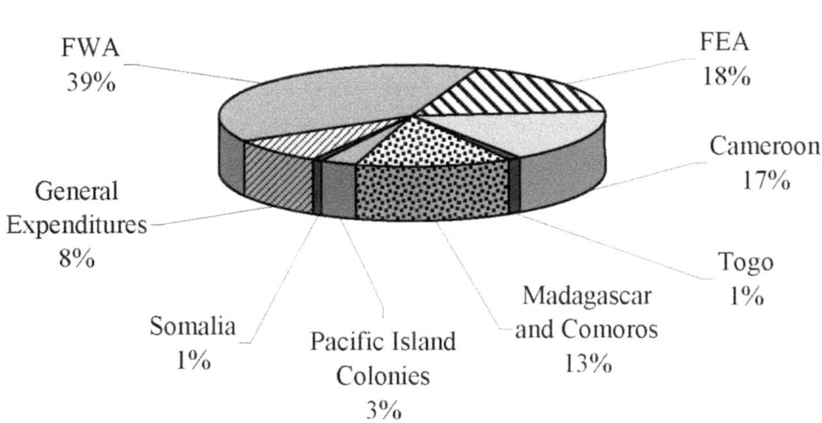

Cameroon: a Privileged Country?

To answer the question of whether Cameroon constituted a privileged country for French overseas public investment, it is first necessary to present the data which make it possible to compare the magnitude of these investments in Cameroon with those made in other French territories in Black Africa, that is to say in French West Africa (FWA), French Equatorial Africa (FEA), Madagascar, and Togo. It is important to note that French West Africa was a group of eight territories that included present-day Benin, Burkina Faso, Côte d'Ivoire, Guinea, Mali, Mauritania, Niger, and Senegal, with almost 20 million inhabitants, and that French Equatorial Africa consisted of four territories including the modern countries of Central African Republic, Chad, Congo, and Gabon, comprising four and a half million inhabitants, as opposed to the approximately three million inhabitants of Cameroon and the approximately one million of Togo.

The following tables provide figures on public investments from the local budgets (table 5.10), CCFOM (table 5.11), the French national budget (table 5.12), and FIDES (table 5.13) made in the territories or groups of territories under French rule.

Table 5.11

Cameroon's contribution to CCFOM investments in Black Africa from 1947 to 1956 (amounts in millions of CFA Francs)

	Cameroon	From an overall total of
1947	80.5	82.5
1948	64.0	418.4
1949	135.6	1,211.4
1950	740.5	2,328.8
1951	1,071.6	3,890.9
1952	1,694.4	6,416.7
1953	1,907.2	4,820.6
1954	749.6	3,732.9
1955	1,453.1	4,305.8
1956	1,847.6	5,257.5

Source: adapted from "Les investissements publics nationaux" vol II, p. 89.

credit granted to Cameroon under this program and the various operations carried out by CCFOM were more than 90 billion French francs by 1955, that is to say nearly 18 percent of the total spending of FIDES during the period. These figures almost equal those for all of French Equatorial Africa which was far more populous and larger, and are greater than those granted to Madagascar. The per capita French contribution is also very significant. "The total of these investments represents a sum of 4,300 CFA Francs per inhabitant. Thus, clearly Cameroon was privileged when compared to the other territories. Indeed, the corresponding number is approximately 2,500 francs for French West Africa, 1,800 for Togo, 3,200 for French Equatorial Africa, and 2,200 for Madagascar."[3]

Considering the information given above, the answer to the question asked earlier can only be in the affirmative: Cameroon indeed enjoyed a favored status with regard to French public overseas investment from 1946 and 1956.

NOTES

1. "Les investissements publics nationaux."
2. "Note d'information de la BCEAO", 39 (October 1958).
3. Didier (H.), "Aperçu sur la situation et l'évolution économique et financière du Cameroun," *La Nouvelle Revue Française d'Outre Mer*, 4 (April 1954): 152.

Chapter 6

Private Investment: a Reality

The Problem of Sources

One is faced with considerable uncertainties when attempting to assess private investment during the period of this study. François Bloch-Lainé bemoaned the lack of statistical data regarding the private sector.[1] As for Pierre Moussa, he wrote that

> Statistical ignorance is even greater for the overseas territories. Thus it is impossible to give a more precise statement in this area than to state that private investment in overseas countries reached several dozen billion francs per year.[2]

Even in the reports of the French financial agency for French Equatorial Africa and Cameroon known as *Institut d'Emission de l'AEF et du Cameroun*, private investment seems to defy analysis:

> The statistical apparatus does not allow us yet to evaluate the importance of private investment with sufficient precision. This is especially true for investments which represent the self-financing of firms which cannot be assessed even approximately.
>
> By contrast, it may be possible to indicate the scale of these investments in the case of operations which show an increase in the capital of already existing companies, as well as in the case of new companies to which credit had been extended. But it is still not possible to determine the amount of capital actually solicited or the portion actually invested.[3]

Why is there such difficulty in quantifying private investment? A partial explanation is provided by Edouard Bonnefous as follows:

> Within the franc zone there is total freedom of capital transfer; thus there are no restrictions at all, not even on the level of statistics, and at the end of the year there appears only a balance sheet which does not enable us to form an idea of the continuing movement of capital. The only valid approximation possible is to quantify the yearly

> performances, inasmuch as these are known. This method obviously does not take into consideration self-financing, local reinvestment of profits and the income derived from cash investments.[4]

In the Cameroonian case, other plausible explanations have emerged in the course of my discussions with other researchers in the country. For example, it seems that it was against the interest of many companies to reveal their profits because of income taxes already in existence at the time. Also, several colonial firms chose to destroy their archives at the time the country attained its independence (January 1, 1960) most likely for racist reasons: they did not want Cameroonians to know about the internal affairs of their businesses.

Thus it is not an easy task to financially assess private investments in Cameroon from 1946 to 1956. This is due to the scarcity of statistical sources, and to the fact that the existing sources are very inaccurate. Nevertheless, some data can be gathered from certain archival documents, mostly consisting of French administrative reports. The use of these documents brings another difficulty to the surface:

> In the case of Cameroon it is impossible to give an exhaustive inventory of the movement of capital to which private investments gave rise. Indeed only foreign investments can be assessed accurately, because of currency controls, and investments which could hope to receive tax exemption.[5]

The majority of the statistical data concerning investment and reinvestment, which influenced the profits of companies and firms relate only to the period between 1946 and 1951. Thus, there are some gray areas, which make it impossible to fully evaluate the entire decade under study.

Financial Assessment

Cross-checking and comparing the amount of the increase in the capital of trading companies, the capital of newly created companies, the development of mid-range and long-term bank credits on the one hand, and, the concrete results these movements may have yielded (importation of equipment, building construction, commercial stock) on the other hand make it possible to estimate the scope of private investment in the territory from 1946 to 1956, at about 14 billion CFA Francs.[6] This constitutes about one fourth of the amount of public investments assessed above. In other words, during the same time period private investment was completely overshadowed by public investment. More precise and complete figures for a longer time period would permit a better understanding of the development of private investment in relation to public investment. Unfortunately, sources do not allow such an analysis beyond 1951.

Table 6.1

Number of private companies according to their type of economic activity in Cameroon in 1950

Type of Activity	Number of Companies
Commerce	120
Animal husbandry	5
Agriculture	136
Mining	38
Forestry	80
Industry	49
Transportation	59
Banks	7
TOTAL	494

Source: Adapted from "Cameroon 1952," *Marchés Coloniaux* (May 17, 1952): 1335.

The estimates given here generally relate to private investment, but it must be understood that the role of foreign capital was extremely feeble. These investments were primarily made by French companies and their subsidiaries in Cameroon, the bulk of local firms, the majority of which were French, and six commercial banks of which five had their headquarters in Paris. CCFOM needs to be added to these banks. It is clear that to talk about private investment in Cameroon is to talk about French private investment.

At the end of 1950 there were 494 private firms and companies in Cameroon. This number does not take into consideration branches or sub-branches of the principal firms. Table 6.1 and figure 6.1 show these private businesses grouped according to their type of economic activity. At the beginning of 1951 there were twenty-eight factories; seven soap factories; and four printing works. In addition, seven hotel-restaurants, seven pharmacies, one shoe factory, two tobacco manufacturers, one oil factory, and one distillery were established in the territory.[7]

It can be seen that the distribution shown above is uneven, and this unevenness does not only concern the distribution according to sectors of activity. The companies were also of unequal importance and wealth. There was an unevenness in terms of geographical distribution too. Almost all of the firms were established in the South. Less than 5 percent of them were to be found in the combined area of the Northern zone and the Adamawa region, even though this area contained more than one third of the territory, and almost 40 percent of the inhabitants of Cameroon. In the South, it was in Douala and in the hinterland of this port city, and in the region of Yaoundé that most firms were established, as one can see in table 6.2.

Table 6.2

Geographical distribution of private firms in Cameroon in 1950.

Regions	Population	Areas	Firms
Wouri (Douala)	3.8%	0.3%	37.2%
Mungo, Nkam and Sanaga Maritime	9.5%	5.7%	15.7%
Nyong et Sanaga (Yaoundé)	13.1%	6.5%	21.5%
Other regions of the South	34.3%	51.7%	20.8%
Adamawa and the North	39.3%	35.8%	4.8%
TOTAL	100%	100%	100%

Source: Adapted from "Cameroun 1952," p. 1272.

Table 6.3

Bank loans to companies in Cameroon from 1949 to 1956.

Year	Loans (amounts in millions of CFA Francs)	Monthly averages
1949	3,548	
1950	4,590	+ 29 %
1951	7,205	+ 57 %
1952	7,041	- 2 %
1953	7,894	+ 12 %
1954	8,925	+ 13 %
1955	10,082	+ 13 %
1956	9,678	- 3.5%

Source: "Note sur la situation économique du territoire à la fin de l'année 1956" (Yaoundé: Territoire du Cameroun, Direction des affaires économiques).

Figure 6.1

Number of private companies according to their type of economic activity in Cameroon in 1950

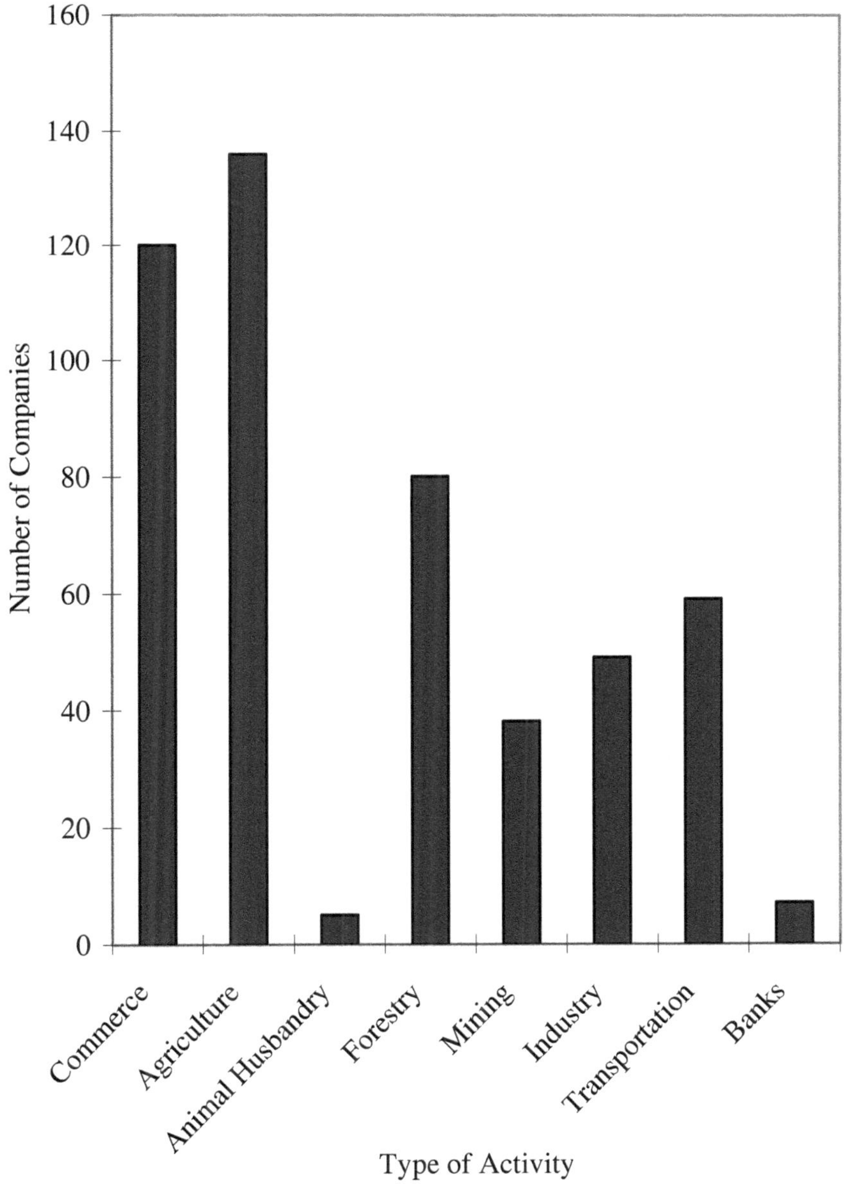

According to Luc de Carbon, who was in charge of research and documentation at CCFOM, the investments of the large commercial and industrial firms, which were active in the whole of the Western and Central African region, represented 400 to 500 million CFA Francs in Cameroon alone. Foreign investments could be assessed at approximately 50 million CFA Francs, and the self-financing of firms and individual investors at 150 million CFA Francs. On June 30, 1951 the amount of private investment in Cameroon was estimated to be approximately 2,500 million CFA Francs.[8] This amount does not include the loans or investments of *Crédit National* or of CCFOM extended under the aegis of specialized research institutes or public bodies to some private companies, either directly or indirectly, and to various companies which had both public and private sources of funds.

For an assessment of private investments in Cameroon, it is necessary to mention the investments which, in the domain of agricultural activity with the support of the advances of the territory and of *Crédit du Cameroun*, have been applied to the development of cash crop and food stuff production.

The role of banks also needs to be considered. Table 6.3 presents the development of bank credits extended to companies between 1949 and 1956, which unfortunately is the only period for which it was possible to find data.

With regard to credit more specifically destined for small companies, cooperatives and individuals, it is interesting to note the activities of *Crédit du Cameroun*, a financial institution that was created in 1949. By June 30, 1953 this organization had distributed 645 million CFA Francs in loans of which 367 million went to cooperatives (that is to say 56 percent of the total); 143 million (22 percent) to real estate operations; 82 million (12 percent) to craftsmen; and 53 million (8 percent) to cultivators.[9]

Data presented in previous tables make it possible to establish that the amount of financial support accorded by CCFOM to private firms by December 30, 1950 was 505.4 million CFA Francs. To this number should be added approximately 200 million in loans included in the loans granted, without specifying their destination, to construction companies which were operating in non-French Africa.

In light of the fact that the loans or advances granted presuppose an equal amount of investment by the concerned firms, and that these investments are only partially comprised in the above assessments, one would arrive at a total private investment in the order of three billion CFA Francs, from 1946 to 1951. This sum does not include agricultural and indigenous urban investments or those coming from autonomous producers whose contributions represent at minimum an equal sum.[10] The sum of approximately three billion was also cited by the Blin Report of 1951, for which this number "has only a relative value" and should not be taken into consideration except with the "strongest reservations." For the compilers of this report, private investment in Cameroon in 1951 was "undeniably of an important volume," and its magnitude was attributed to two causes, namely:

> To the importance of the profit margins realized since 1946, thanks to the constant rise in the price of imported goods and the currency rate prevailing for export goods, one part of which in any case should be attributed to monetary manipulations; furthermore to the impact of public investment which gives rise to temporary activity, securing direct profits on the import of construction materials and equipment destined to be invested, and indirect profits on the importation of consumer goods the volume of

Table 6.4

Declared profits of the largest firms of Cameroon from 1946 to 1950 (amounts in CFA Francs)

	1946	1947	1948
		French Firms	
F	30,006,967	83,882,990	110,185,856
X	15,478,841	33,282,240	46,175,222
L	3,932,143	6,845,300	9,053,454
LLL	4,686,792	17,983,251	6,358,086
AA	3,481,681	3,380,547	3,362,674
MMM	Creation	Loss	106,000
DDD	No Document	No Document	11,187,000
NNN	Loss	Loss	4,149,270
OOO	Loss	Loss	1,163,679
PPP	Loss	1,332,133	1,805,192
QQQ	Loss	Loss	3,699,021
G	920,000	3,109,062	4,023,377
RRR	14,023,000	27,630,000	43,543,000
		Foreign Firms	
U		5,005,029	12,081,878
E	19,083,284	43,214,531	67,538,983
Z	8,751,372	15,669,719	34,988,321
I	1,872,889	1,869,000	21,122,918
J	3,713,150	12,535,285	11,689,795
P	484,486	3,043,920	6,527,155
SSS	5,923,658	2,238,924	3,270,826
TOTAL	112,000,000	260,000,000	301,000,000

Table 6.4 *(Continued)*

	1949	1950
	French Firms	
F	136,368,724	241,869,295
X	97,402,860	107,159,139
L	16,403,758	8,536,652
LLL	6,922,496	4,593,255
AA	No data	10,100,000
MMM	3,108,500	6,384,316
DDD	19,841,000	No data
NNN	1,353,600	924,752
OOO	3,047,567	Loss
PPP	1,260,971	3,656,157
QQQ	99,571	1,569,181
G	17,447,455	21,286.907
RRR	100,683,000	86,000,000
	Foreign Firms	
U	56,230,084	35,931,252
E	116,749,253	187,797,618
Z	65,933,116	93,864,000
I	9,972,316	28,183,133
J	68,163,140	66,588,993
P	12,375,601	28,544,245
SSS	3,206,592	2,096,217
TOTAL	737,000,000	936,000,000

Source: ANSOM, affaires économiques 85, Rapport Blin.

> which even increased thanks to the means of payment distributed in the country due to the profits derived from FIDES activities.[11]

Private investment first of all benefited the "largest firms." It is impossible, however, to refer to these "large firms" by name, because their names do not appear except in code in the documents used for this study, perhaps because of the "top secret" nature of the document. Table 6.4 shows the statements of income of twenty of Cameroon's largest firms from 1946 to 1950, chosen from different fields of activity. This table does not include state and semi-public companies. These firms reinvested little of their profits in Cameroon. According to the Blin Report, only 20 percent of the profits had been reinvested. The assessment of reinvestments was based on tax statements, and demands for tax relief on the reinvested sums made by companies and individuals. Table 6.5 lists the reinvestments made by the principal firms of Cameroon from 1946 to 1950. Reinvestments by secondary firms are shown in table 6.6.

Table 6.5

Reinvestment in Cameroon by the principal firms from 1946 to 1950 (amounts in thousands of CFA Francs)

	1946	1947	1948	1949	1950	TOTAL
O				6,000	4,415	10,415
P			3,327	5,914	7,896	17,137
Z			9,617		7,940	17,557
U					7,557	7,557
E		4,685	11,528	7,951	4,791	28,995
Q		2,500	5,620	4,000		12,120
R		1,340	1,990	2,607	1,290	7,227
S			11,000	32,247	55,466	98,713
J		1,086	2,376	14,781		18,243
AA		2,960	950	8,746	23,807	36,458
BB				21,000	15,015	36,000
L			8,000	20,106	23,182	51,288
X				6,897	2,514	9,411
K				16,930	8,970	25,900
W				19,399	5,620	25,019
CC					14,540	14,540
H	1,897	5,411	12,695	19,195	29,901	69,099
DD	1,171	2,223	7,334	13,367	18,096	42,191
EE	20,226	31,200	27,300	16,944		95,670
FF		4,116	1,470	3,862	3,857	13,305
GG		1,390	2,895	12,240	22,199	39,724
HH					12,233	12,233
TOTAL						687,762

Source: ANSOM, affaires économiques 85, Rapport Blin.

Table 6.6

Reinvestment in Cameroon by secondary firms from 1946 to 1950 (amounts in CFA Francs)

Firms	Amounts
II	13,638,000
JJ	3,500,000
KK	17,729,000
MM	40,696,000
NN	14,506,000
N	3,475,000
A	5,093,000
OO	13,706,000
PP	3,913,000
I	8,446,000
QQ	4,093,000
RR	14,728,000
SS	7,545,000
TT	5,706,000
UU	24,014,000
VV	8,753,000
WW	11,487,000
LL	12,019,000
TOTAL	213,043,000

Source: ANSOM, affaires économiques 85, Rapport Blin.

From 1946 to 1950 the total reinvestment of the profits made by private firms in Cameroon was 1,341,850,000 CFA Francs, of which 686,762,000 francs (51.25 percent of the total) were made by major firms, 213,041,000 francs (15.87 percent) by secondary firms; 441,040,000 francs (32.86 percent) constitute reinvestment of secondary significance.

Reinvestment was made in various sectors of the economy. However, an analysis of this reinvestment by sector shows an uneven distribution, as can be seen from table 6.7 and figure 6.2. The most striking case is that of the banking and commercial sector. With 790 million CFA Francs, that is to say nearly 60 percent of all reinvestment, this sector is the one that reinvested the most from 1946 to 1950. The industrial sector was in second position with about 15 percent of reinvestment, but far behind banking and commerce. Agriculture followed with about 8 percent; forestry, garages and workshops, with approximately 7 percent each; and finally the soap factories, with about 4 percent.

Table 6.7

Breakdown by sector of private reinvestment in Cameroon from 1946 to 1950

Sectors	Amounts (in CFA Francs)
Commerce and banks	790,000,000
Industries	200,000,000
Agriculture	110,000,000
Garages and workshops	90,000,000
Forestry	90,000,000
Soap manufacturing	60,000,000

Source: ANSOM, affaires économiques 85, Rapport Blin.

Figure 6.2

Distribution by sector of private reinvestment in Cameroon from 1946 to 1950

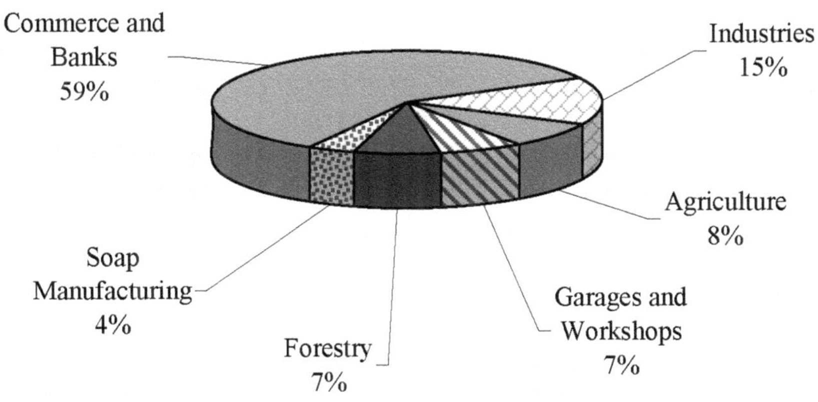

Table 6.8

Investments made in Cameroon in 1951 and 1952 by new companies or with new capital.

Companies	Amounts (in CFA Francs)
Agriculture	
SPROA	120,000,000
Société Palme	30,000,000
SEITA	50,000,000
SRC	100,000,000
SIC	160,000,000
Pitoa – Bertoua	35,000,000
Bastos	10,000,000
Forestry	
CFC Yansoki	900,000,000
LBC Eséka	600,000,000
Industry	
Société Africaine de textile	400,000,000
Brasseries du Cameroun	180,000,000
SOCACI	40,000,000
Air liquide	65,000,000
Valor Brossette	200,000,000
CARIC	120,000,000
SATEI	50,000,000
BAUDON	30,000,000
CFPDA Douala	100,000,000
Shell Garoua	50,000,000
CEA and CEAC	140,000,000
CCDEE	90,000,000
TOTAL	3,570,000,000

Source: ANCAM, 2AC 9812.

The significance of the banking and commercial sector during this period springs from the needs created by the provision of necessary infrastructure. Actually, the execution of certain projects and the provision of necessary equipment led to increasing commercial activities and banking transactions.

The infrastructural development in itself made the development of other economic sectors possible.

It should be noted that the above breakdown is arbitrary. Actually, companies did not necessarily reinvest in their own principal branch of activity. Indeed many industrial or agricultural firms reinvested in residential or commercial real estate.

The above estimates refer to reinvestments made from 1946 to 1950 by companies already installed in Cameroon. In 1951 and 1952 a new trend began: it was no longer a question of reinvestment but rather of investment by companies which until then had not been present in Cameroon; the bulk of these investments tended to drive up those of existing companies, as can be seen in table 6.8 which represents investments by new companies or by pre-existing companies receiving an injection of cash. The total which appears in this table includes 500 to 600 million CFA Francs of funds pledged but not actually spent.

The above estimates made the French authorities conclude that private investment existed and that its amount was satisfactory. But in actuality, these investments were not all that satisfactory, and as time passed they continued to diminish. Significantly, efforts were made by the French Government to increase private investment and reinvestment in Black Africa in general and Cameroon in particular.

The Policy of Persuasion or Incentives for Private Investment and Reinvestment

The Brazzaville Conference of 1944 recommended that the development of Africa and especially its industrialization be, in general, made by private companies. The administration was only to aid private initiatives "by assuming the costs of pilot plants whose importance it recognized, during their trial period; by maintaining industries which were vital for the country although operating at a loss; by creating testing plants and research centers placed at the disposal of industrialists for all studies or manufacturing control."[12]

Public investment was to play a stimulating role. However, this direct intervention of the Government, especially in the realm of infrastructural investment, did not have the desired effect of persuading private concerns to invest overseas even though "the development of production in the overseas territories appeared...to be one of the most certain means of facilitating the development of these territories and of improving the living standards of its inhabitants."[13]

The actual significance of this public effort must not, however, be overestimated. If it was important by comparison to the internal effort, it nonetheless remained objectively weak by comparison with the needs. In 1953 Ivan du Jonchay compared this public effort of France in the overseas territories with French public investment support to France's national electric company known as *Electricité de France (EDF)*:

> If we compare (French investment in Africa) to metropolitan investment, we find that in five years France invested more than 4,000 billion, but out of this total the territories outside of the *métropole* only received 760 billion, which roughly equals *Electricité de France* (700); during the same period, metropolitan coal-mining cost 458 billion, and the French railways 182 billion.[14]

Thus, if the goals of the equipment and development plans of the French overseas areas were to be met, this insufficiency of public investment demanded the massive contribution of private capital. Unfortunately, the reconstruction needs of France and the other European countries in the aftermath of the Second World War offered better remuneration for French and foreign capital within the *métropole* and within Europe. Indeed the reconstruction effort and the rapid development it generated offered a very high rate of profit and a great degree of security to private capital, then rare in Europe. Also, private companies preferred to invest in Europe, rather than take risks and cope with uncertainties in Africa, where the losses experienced by colonial firms during the War loomed large in the minds of investors. Hence the weakness of overseas private investment, as highlighted by a report of the *Commissariat Général au Plan de Modernisation et d'Equipement* for the 1947–1951 period.

> Private capital did not meet the expectations of State investments. The feasibility of the Trust Fund to grant aid to certain private firms has made possible the priming and then the preservation of a flow of capital towards the overseas territories, but it is a relatively weak flow. The depression of the metropolitan financial market, the many risks affecting the creation of production firms overseas, and the high personnel costs along with other factors explain the insufficiency of private investment.[15]

It is clear, then, that the lack of private investment became a problem for the French Government whose overseas development plan was in danger of failing completely unless a massive infusion of private capital arrived. To remedy the situation, a series of additional incentives were needed to create favorable conditions for companies to establish themselves and to ensure their smooth functioning overseas.

In Cameroon measures were taken to increase private investment and reinvestment. One of these measures was Resolution No. 66 which was passed on April 13, 1950 by ARCAM. This law provided for an additional tax of 10 percent from the profits of companies not reinvesting in Cameroon.[16] Another measure was embodied in Order No. 3206 of July 4, 1956 which granted a large tax exemption to new industries.[17]

In Paris, Article 32 of the *Loi des Finances* (Finance Law) of December 31, 1953 was to give a push to the new policy of persuasion. Law No. 531336, which was one of the many laws accompanying *Loi des Finances* No. 531308 of December 31, 1953, concerned the special accounts of the Treasury for the year 1954, and actually stipulated in its Article 32 that:

> For those production companies whose creation, equipment or extension has special significance for the implementation of the modernization plan of the territories where they carry out their activities, the councils and local assemblies of the overseas territories will grant a long-term program which will guarantee them the stability of all or part of the tax expenses they have to bear.
> The applicability of a special long-term tax system to authorized firms will be limited to a maximum period of 15 years, including the period of their establishment. A regulation of the public administration based on the report of the Minister of Overseas France or of Finance will determine the conditions of application of the provisions of the present Article.[18]

The regulation of the public administration intended for the application of Article 32 was to come into effect on June 4, 1954 by Decree No. 54573. It stipulated that the authorization order, issued jointly by the Ministers of Overseas France and of Finance, must define the goals and the program of equipment of a firm as well as its eventual obligations. The councils and local assemblies were to determine the characteristics of the categories of firms affected by this decree. In case an approved company were to default in meeting the obligations imposed by the authorization, the agreement would be withdrawn and the company would be subject to the general tax laws.[19]

It was in keeping with the new policy of persuasion decided by Paris, that ATCAM adopted the provisions, which allowed the establishment in Cameroon of ALUCAM Péchiney-Ugine, one of the most important French projects in the territory. The ALUCAM project, meant a modification in the tax system, the general code of direct taxation, and the registration fees throughout the territory. To encourage significant investment, the length of tax exempt status was extended from three to five years. The tax rates were augmented by a progressive tapering of rates for aspects of production including machines, skilled personnel, unskilled labor, power generation, and tonnage of transported goods. The stability of the tax system was guaranteed for fifteen years for electro-chemical and electro-metallurgical firms and for companies producing electricity, provided that they would be constituted in the form of local companies and that they would show proof of producing 50 kw (kilowatts) of electricity. The benefits of this system were extended to companies whose activity in Cameroon was linked to those of local companies.[20]

Article 32 of Law 531336, which created the "long-term tax system," had to be significantly modified after the *Loi Cadre* (Outline Law) of June 23, 1956 was passed. This modification mainly concerned the duration of the agreement period for the establishment of a business: "the applicability of the long-term tax system to the authorized firms will be limited to a maximum period of twenty five years, increased if need be by five years, the normal installation period." This is how the report accompanying Decree 561132 of November 13, 1956 justified the modification:

> Studies concerning the development of the energy and mining resources of the overseas territories show that on the one hand the period of the establishment of operating companies could be rather long and that on the other hand the nature and magnitude of the projected installations call for long depreciation periods.
>
> As a result, it is desirable that the maximum duration of the implementation period of the long-term tax system be extended to twenty-five years for this category of firms and that this period should further be augmented by the normal installation delays.[21]

Moreover in 1956 many decrees concerning overseas territories were passed. On November 13, under the joint initiative of the Overseas Ministry and the Ministry of Finance, sixteen decrees were issued, of which at least ten directly concerned economic questions and particularly the question of private investment.[22] They constituted a set of measures aimed at assuring appreciably improved conditions of remuneration and depreciation for companies, and low production costs to allow them to be competitive internationally. The introductory statement of one of these decrees mentioned the following:

> One of the best ways to fulfill these conditions and to persuade companies to invest consists of assuring the most important companies as stable conditions for their functioning as possible....Indeed, everybody knows that in any case these companies remain subject to the risks engendered by the economic conjuncture and to technical problems against which there are no guarantees.
>
> The most important conditions of the normal functioning of companies are free trade, the ease of recruitment of their personnel, the ease of acquiring the raw materials which they need on the best possible terms, and the respect of the equality of the firms and of their partners. This is why agreements can make sure that the territory will not be able to oppose the signing and execution of contracts relating to the sale and shipping of the products of the firm, and that it will facilitate the import of raw materials and equipment necessary for its functioning.[23]

Clearly, the French Government made efforts to stimulate private investment and reinvestment in Cameroon. However, a number of questions could be asked. For example, did the policy of persuasion implemented by the colonial state with regard to private investment attain its declared objectives? Did the steps taken by the French authorities to remedy the lack of private investment prevent private disinvestment? The next chapter will provide answers to these questions.

NOTES

1. Bloch-Lainé (F.), p. 415.
2. Moussa (P.), *Les chances économiques de la communauté franco-africaine* (Paris: A.Colin, 1957), p. 127.
3. "Institut d'Emission de l'AEF et du Cameroun. Rapport d'activité," fiscal year 1957, p. 34.
4. Bonnefous (E.), p. 42.
5. ANSOM, FIDES 351, "Le plan et l'évolution du Cameroun, 1947–1956," p. 106.
6. *Ibid.*
7. "Cameroun 1952," *Marchés Coloniaux* (May 17, 1952): 1335.
8. Carbon (L. de), "Le crédit et l'organisation bancaire," *Marchés Coloniaux* (May 17, 1952): 1335.
9. Didier (H.), "Aperçu sur la situation et l'évolution économiques et financières du Cameroun," *La Nouvelle Revue Française d'Outre mer*, 4 (April 1954): 152.
10. Carbon (L. de), p. 1335.
11. ANSOM, affaires économiques 85, Rapport Blin.
12. *La Conférence Africaine Française*, p. 51.
13. Introductory report to the Decree 56 1133 of November 13, 1956 concerning long-term conventions likely to be passed with certain categories of overseas firms (*JORF, lois et décrets*, 1956, p. 10916).
14. Du Jonchay (I.), *L'industrialisation de l'Afrique* (Paris: Payot, 1953), pp. 269–270.
15. "Cinq ans d'exécution du plan de modernisation et d'équipement de l'Union française. Réalisations 1947–1951 et programme 1952" (Paris: Commissariat Général au Plan de Modernisation et d'Equipement, 1952, p. 245).
16. ANSOM, affaires économiques 85, Rapport Blin.
17. *Journal Officiel du Cameroun* (July 11, 1954). See also "Cameroun 1952," p. 241.
18. *JORF, lois et décrets* (January 5, 1954): 241.
19. *JORF, lois et décrets* (1956): 10915.
20. *Climats*, No. 448, 15–21 juillet 1954, p. 7.
21. *JORF, lois et décrets* (1956): 10915.
22. All these decrees are listed in *JORF, lois et décrets* (1956): 10915.
23. *JORF, lois et décrets* (1956): 10916. On the incentives to private investment in French Black Africa, see also: "Avantages et garanties accordés aux investissements en Afrique française au sud du Sahara" (Ministère de la France d'Outre Mer, Direction des affaires économiques et du plan); Lawrence (A.), "Les investissements dans les territoires d'outre mer," *JORF, Conseil Economique, avis et rapports* (March 7, 1956): 105–135.

Chapter 7

Private Investment: a Myth

Failure of the Policy of Persuasion

There is evidence clearly showing that private disinvestment affected Cameroon from the early 1950s. For example, table 3.1 (see chapter 3) shows that between 1951 and 1953, the number of new firms and firms increasing their capital investment decreased from 142 to 134 while the capital investment decreased from 1,592.5 to 1,041.7 million CFA Francs. The figures of table 7.1 are also revealing.

Table 7.1

Transfers of private capital between Cameroon and the franc zone from 1949 to 1953 (amounts in millions of CFA Francs)

		1949	1950	1951	1952	1953
Bank transfers	Receipts	1,779	2,059	6,533	10,730	11,061
	Payments	3,872	3,636	12,468	15,557	15,264
	Balance	-2,930	-1,577	-5,935	-4,827	-4,203
Postal orders and transfers by check	Receipts	69	76	98	139	142
	Payments	494	882	1,099	1,262	1,218
	Balance	-425	-806	-1,001	-1,122	-1,076

Source: *Bulletin Mensuel de Statistiques Coloniales.*

Figure 7.1

Transfers of private capital between Cameroon and the franc zone from 1949 to 1953

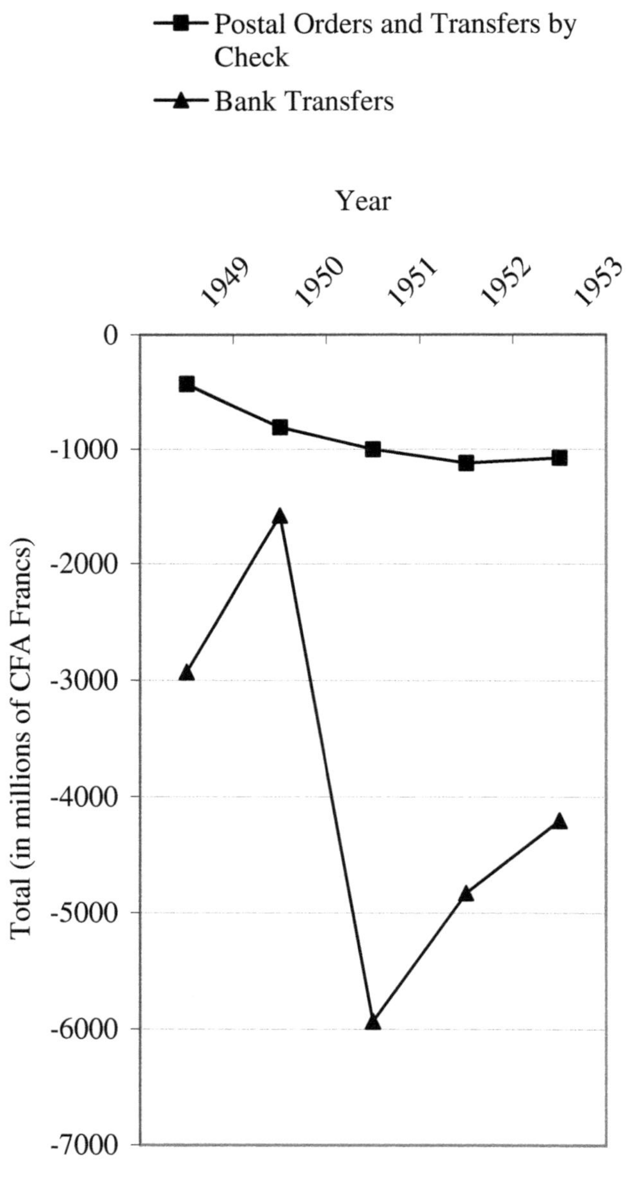

This table and figure 7.1, show the transfer of private funds between Cameroon, on the one hand, and France and the rest of the franc zone, on the other. The operations considered here are bank transfers (with the exception of the Treasury in conjunction with CCFOM), postal orders and check transfers. In these areas, the numbers that appear in this table show a constant and growing deficit that characterized Cameroon between 1949 and 1953, which unfortunately is the only period for which sources are available.

The balance shows a deficit during the entire period under scrutiny both for bank transfers and postal orders and checks. This deficit grew every year from 1950 on. It rose from -1,577 million CFA Francs in 1950 to -5,935 million in 1951 and to -4,203 million in 1953 for bank transfers, and from -425 million CFA Francs in 1950 to -1,076 million in 1953 in the case of postal transfers. All these data bear witness to the retreat of private capital from Cameroon in the 1950s.

In 1951 it was still possible to talk of the influx of capital to Cameroon. Afterwards, this influx became rarer and rarer, as noted by a writer in the colonial press who was inspired by a description by Robert Buron:

> Economic development is not what it should be, new funds trickle in and private investment accounts for 9/10th of the reinvestment of already existing companies.[1]

The industrial domain was the most affected by private disinvestment. In fact, with the exception of *Société Industrielle des Cacaos* created in 1954, no new industry was established in Cameroon after 1951. The only significant industrial investments were made with semi-public funds, which shows that public investment compensated for private disinvestment. Many small firms founded during that period were not very important, and some ceased to function. After the liquidation of *Compagnie Française du Cameroun* and *Compagnie des Industries Forestières du Cameroun*, the closing of the *Nassif* factories, the difficulties encountered by *Bois du Cameroun* in 1952, the weakness of the sales of *Energie Electrique du Cameroun*, and the problems revealed by the appointment of a manager for the oil-works of Dibombari, the outlook for industrialization in Cameroon seemed gloomy.

In lumber-related industries only one company really benefited while the others registered more or less significant losses for several years. While the wood industries operated at a loss, the situation of rubber remained precarious due to the weakness of world prices. In a variety of industries with the exception of some particularly profitable ones, the situation was very often difficult. In construction businesses several local entrepreneurs found themselves practically bankrupt. Although three large companies, namely *Meunier-Cameroun, Egica* and *Monod* were forced to abandon the territory, the situation of the remaining entrepreneurs did not improve at all and there were several bankruptcies. Many carpenters in the territory were similarly faced with very considerable difficulties. Metal industries and industries related to bridge construction suffered from a chronic lack of demand. The hotel industry was also affected; in Douala alone two hotels, though long established, and several restaurants had to close their doors at the end of 1954 and in early 1955. Finally, the large number of retail stores led to excessive competition among small traders, which was harmful to them.[2]

In summary, private investment projects were reduced and only operated weakly, with the exception of cement works which were assured of a market. In contrast to the still flourishing agricultural production the industrial situation was tense. Many industries actually survived on loans granted to them by public institutions or investment banks. In the mid 1950s industry was in a state of near-failure in Cameroon, especially in the South:

> In the south of Cameroon industrialization is at a standstill....Bassa which was intended to become a significant industrial center saw the creation of a cocoa butter factory and a cement factory, after the soap factory of the CCC. These three industries, the oil depots and the railway workshops, are all that have actually been realized even though industry was supposed to grow there, as it was announced five years ago, like mushrooms after rain.[3]

Thus it cannot be said that the measures taken by the French authorities to encourage French private investment really achieved their objectives. The private disinvestment which began in French overseas territories in the early 1950s continued irrevocably. The consequences affected the economies of these territories to varying degrees. In 1955, the economic situation of Cameroon was on the whole much more favorable than that of many other overseas territories.[4]

The economic stagnation of the overseas territories can also be explained by the "currency trafficking" or the "CFA Franc scandal." In 1953, superintendent Néant of the Criminal Investigation Department of Paris, who specialized in currency trafficking, was put in charge of an investigation of a widespread traffic in CFA Francs, French francs, and dollars which had certainly been in existence for a long time. This traffic involved the entire CFA zone, but especially Cameroon. Many foreign traders, as well as rich Hausa merchants and chiefs were involved in it. The numbers that were given about this traffic were both unbelievable and imprecise: for the entire CFA zone the traffic involved tens of billions by the end of 1953. According to the French press, especially *France-Soir* whose analyses were republished by *Le Cameroun Libre*, the police report determined that the French territories of Africa were on the brink of economic stagnation due to the activities of some traffickers; the beneficiaries were the neighboring British colonies.[5]

The trafficking originated because of the existing disparity between the prices in the British colonies and those in the French colonies, the former being lower than the latter. To supply oneself in the British territories, pound sterlings were needed. It was at this point that the traffickers intervened. With a compensation system and for a commission of 1 to 2 percent they obtained the pounds for the interested parties which could be transferred to any British bank. "The mechanism of the traffic consisted of a succession of exchanges from the CFA Franc; CFA Franc was converted into French Franc and the latter was exchanged in France into pound sterling, on the black market."[6]

This traffic had disastrous consequences: the position of the franc weakened; French industry suffered from competition against which it could not fight on equal footing and the profit thus made escaped taxation; Cameroon and other African countries suffered from capital flight which harmed their economies and their development prospects.

The currency trafficking makes the assessment of the movements of capital between Cameroon and France very difficult. Although it helps understand the withdrawal of private capital from Cameroon, it cannot entirely account for this process. There are other factors that can explain private disinvestment and the reluctance of foreign capital to move towards the territory.

The Causes of Private Disinvestment

Financial Causes

Financial and political causes contributed to the private disinvestment which affected Cameroon during the 1950s. Financially, two factors seem to have been of the greatest importance: the instability of the CFA Franc; and the crippling tax system which weighed upon investment in Cameroon, especially on small firms.

During the period under consideration, the CFA Franc had been devalued several times: first on December 26, 1945; and second on January 26, 1948. The latter devaluation led to dissatisfaction among Cameroonian politicians. For example, Soppo Priso declared at the Assembly of the French Union of which he was a member, that Cameroon because of circumstances, found itself "especially wronged," that the poor Cameroonian consumer felt that he was "more penalized than his French brother," and that the devaluation was a "matter of life and death" for the country. Then in agreement with all the other deputies of the territory he presented a proposition which stipulated the following:

> The Assembly of the French Union after having become aware of the devaluation of certain colonial francs, in particular of the CFA franc of Cameroon protests against this unwarranted devaluation....
> Invites the Government to maintain the exchange rate with the US dollar and the pound such as it existed on January 1, 1948 without a bonus of 80 percent upon buying or selling.[7]

Cameroonians were not the only ones to express their discontent over the devaluation of the CFA Franc. Protests also came from the other territories of French Africa. Paul Coste-Floret, Minister of Overseas France had to provide an explanation. In a speech given at the congress of the *Mouvement Républicain Populaire* (MRP) at Toulouse, he stated:

> We had to devaluate the CFA Franc. There is no doubt about this. This is a very heavy sacrifice for the population of Black Africa. Moreover...I also know that the devaluation of the CFA Franc is not even beneficial for the *métropole* itself....Although it does not benefit the overseas territories taken separately, and it does not favor the *métropole* either when taken alone, the devaluation was necessary when we take the French Union as a whole. If we wanted to bring conclusive technical solutions to the problems we were faced with, the disparity between the economic conditions of the territories of Black Africa would have forced us to introduce in each territory different monetary units and to create a veritable mosaic of colonial francs. This would clearly have meant the end of the French Union at the very moment that we are about to build it. This is why we devaluated the CFA Franc and I continue to believe that this remains a valid reason.[8]

The CFA Franc was subsequently devalued again on October 18, 1948, and on September 20, 1949. These successive devaluations and the constant rumors of further devaluations became a veritable psychosis, among both investors and the overseas deputies, as noted by a representative of the colonial press who was himself opposed to the government's decision:

> From time to time a delegation of overseas deputies, in the name of the defense committee of the CFA Franc, visits either the Ministry of Overseas France or the Ministry of Finance to demand clarification about a rumor of the devaluation of the CFA Franc. The minister receives the delegation, presents an official denial of the alleged rumor.... The delegation departs, with the communiqué. A fortnight later new rumor, new delegation, new denial, new assurances, etc.
> This scenario has become well known...it is not enough to make the CFA into a stable currency, which is the first requirement of a currency....
> Give more concrete guarantees to this franc than the ones granted to it on its birth certificate which can easily be transformed into a death certificate by the stroke of a pen. As long as the CFA Franc is likely to die overnight without any further ado, it will only inspire very relative confidence....
> It is time to grant Africa a currency based on real and solid foundations.[9]

Besides the devaluations of the CFA Franc, there were also the many changes in the parity between the CFA Franc and the metropolitan franc. One of the most frequent complaints against the CFA Franc was that it was created by a simple notice of the *Office des Changes* (exchange bureau), and that its parity was contingent on a new notice which had the power to alter overnight the 2 to 1 rate established in 1944 between the CFA Franc and the Metropolitan Franc. Many deputies suggested that in order to avoid surprises this parity should be modifiable only by a law, and not by a simple notice of the *Office des Changes.*[10] During the Economic Conference of the Franc Zone, organized on May 12 in Casablanca, by the *Comité d'Etude et de Liaison du Patronat de l'Union Française*, business circles expressed their reaction:

> (The Conference) wants the CFA Franc to be abolished and replaced by francs equivalent to the metropolitan franc, without any loss to the bearers or holders of the CFA Franc. A variety of practical measures for the exchange were envisaged. In any case it seems necessary that the Government take steps, because the persistent rumors of the devaluation of the CFA Franc, despite all the denials, constitute considerable difficulties in business and slow down investments.[11]

The French authorities were aware of these reactions and of the difficulties the persistent rumors of devaluation and changes in the parity caused for private investors. In 1953, Schweitzer, Director of the Treasury, expressed his regret that it was difficult to find an efficient way of stopping all these persistent rumors about a new devaluation. He also stated that he was unable to declare that the rate of the CFA will not be touched.[12] The French Government made declarations with a view to reassuring everyone. Talking at the National Assembly in 1949, Tony Revillon, State Secretary of Finance reiterated "as clearly as possible, so that there is no more ambiguity" that the Government was not going to modify the rate of the CFA Franc in relation to the metropolitan franc.[13] A few years later, in 1954, the French Government made another declaration through Robert Buron, Minister of Overseas France, who stated that:

> The extremely clear, and extremely precise, and altogether irrevocable affirmation, that the actual 1 to 2 ratio between the metropolitan franc and the CFA Franc is and remains unchanged. The Minister of Finance and myself are in absolute agreement on this point: there can be no question of causing trouble in the workings of overseas economies by manipulating currency rates....
>
> The current Government cannot do anything with regard to the CFA Franc, but affirms even more emphatically the inviolable character of this parity. We must definitely stop this kind of chronic fear that ceaselessly drains our overseas territories by the systematic and premature return of capital towards the *métropole*. We must have confidence in the unity of all the French people; each and everyone must know that their resources

are as totally secure in Dakar, in Abidjan, in Yaoundé or in Tananarive, as in Paris itself.[14]

The intervention of the French authorities had no effect. Between 1950 and 1957 the CFA Franc was not devalued, and the parity between this franc and the French Franc remained unchanged. However, the attitude of private investors during this time did not change. The instability of the CFA Franc contributed to slowing down the development of private investment as A. Lawrence explained in a report on "investments in the overseas territories" presented to the Economic Council in January 1956:

> If we look at things from the point of view of the investor, we must acknowledge that there is a fear that the parity between the CFA Franc and the metropolitan franc will be modified. The existence of a doubt on the question of the longevity of the rate between the CFA Franc and the metropolitan franc no doubt constitutes one of the most potent slow downs of private investment.
>
> Bank and postal transfers in general show a negative balance sheet. It seems that civil servants, private companies, and even the public sector, are sending back their holdings to the *métropole,* in order to avoid substantial losses in case of devaluation.[15]

In addition to the uncertainties surrounding the CFA Franc, the "crushing tax system" constituted another reason for the private disinvestment by small investors and traders. After the period of euphoria (1950–1953), it was officially acknowledged in Cameroon that new tax burdens would be unbearable and fatal to the economy of the territory. Thus the territorial assembly of Cameroon (ATCAM) decided that there would not be any new taxes. However some understood this to mean an acceleration in the rate of tax collection, and a blow to small and medium size firms and to small trade which would be crushed by the costs. Here is an example provided by a local newspaper, *L'Eveil du Cameroun*:

> The first case we shall cite is that of a small trader whose annual turnover is 5 million francs.
>
> It is acknowledged that the profit margin is 20 percent that is to say 1 million francs. Let's see what taxes lower this sum:
>
> Tax on turnover/sales: 60% 300,000
> Tax on industrial and commercial profit 180,000
> General additional tax on revenue: 10% 82,000
> Employer contribution to professional training and
> solidarity tax; vaccinal tax: around 10% 26,000
> Total: .... 588,000 that is to say 58.80% in taxes.
>
> We should not be surprised then by the ever increasing number of bankruptcies in the territory![16]

The following testimony of Pierre Ngayewang, a Cameroonian businessman, is also very interesting:

> Honest taxpayers feel themselves strangled by tax authorities; crushed under the weight of taxes, they wonder what they could do to help in the recovery toward a healthy economy in the country.... What is most disturbing, is that "the regulation was applied arbitrarily" without taking into consideration the precarious nature of the finances of the African taxpayer who finds himself today materially incapable of paying up accumulated late taxes. And under the pretext of stabilizing the market, we are in the middle of the systematic elimination of the small trader who is slowly being killed.[17]

Even more than the Cameroonians, the *colons* (settlers) of Cameroon, whose significance for the economic life of the territory was well known, denounced the ravages of the fiscal policy of the local administration:

> Firms collapse under the weight of these charges. One after the other, those who don't have a sufficiently solid base cease their activity. Others declare bankruptcy or take advantage of court-supervised liquidations. More and more signs: "Store for rent" can be seen.... The crisis is growing, all bets are off.
>
> The number of firms is constantly diminishing, and as a result all the costs tend to devolve on the remaining few firms; some of these in turn fall too, and so on and so forth. The vicious cycle continues.
>
> There is no sign of...any new industries (in Douala, in the industrial center of Bassa).... We don't see anything coming.
>
> Neither metropolitan nor foreign capital will take risks in countries where the economy is collapsing under the weight of all kinds of charges and where the already existing businesses fail one after the other.
>
> Thus the situation is simple. No investment, the elimination of even more new firms, not because they are not healthy...but because there comes a moment when taxes kill, and when the costs become intolerable. New bankruptcies are in sight, decline in the progressive economic and even social development, the worsening of unemployment in the centers, growing cost of living affecting primarily the rural masses, the production costs of goods increasing further due to the charges weighing on transportation, with some products unable to support these costs.
>
> And all this because one must at all cost find the necessary resources to maintain an administrative machine which has become a monster, a veritable greedy Moloch.[18]

It was by means of the *Conférence des Petites et Moyennes Entreprises* (CPME—Conference of Small and Medium Size Firms) that the *colons*, during a meeting which took place in Yaoundé on July 3, 1955, also criticized the tardiness of the Administration in settling its debts. For the CPME, this situation was particularly harmful to all, and especially to small and medium size firms since some of them were obliged to fold. The CPME demanded not only a quick settling of the outstanding bills of the administration, but also a lowering of the excessive tax rates, not merely a stop to their growth.[19] Finally, the white settlers considered unjust the granting of special tax benefits to new companies only.

> In order to attract capital to Cameroon, special tax benefits have been granted to new firms, which favor them considerably by comparison to firms which had established themselves here when big companies were not willing to take risks. This is already a flagrant injustice. But these are French firms. It is likely that such advantages would not have dare been granted to foreign businesses and assets if French capital which had been invested for a long time had not benefited from them.
> One suspects that foreign investors are well informed and aware of this situation. They know that in comparison with the privileged new businesses they are handicapped, and they have to work under much less favorable circumstances.
> Thus, by granting such tax benefits to the said privileged firms through long-term advantages, the new foreign investors are faced with yet another hurdle. All the more reason why they should not be counted on as, "pioneering capital."...
> The privileges of reduced taxation granted to the new, French firms allowing them to compete victoriously with the old, established firms, could very well have been a miscalculation as well as an injustice.[20]

From the evidence above it can be concluded that the tax policy of Cameroon in the 1950s constituted one of the negative factors which hindered the development of private capitalism in the territory, inasmuch as this policy provoked the failure of several local firms without being able to attract new investors. The instability of the CFA Franc was also presented as one of the contributing factors to private disinvestment in the territory. But financial factors are not sufficient to explain this disinvestment. There were also causes of a political nature which help to understand the otherwise seemingly incomprehensible behaviors.

Political Causes

In a work which he published in 1957, H. Durand evoked "the political instability which predominated in the overseas French Union, an instability to which Black Africa was also subject, and which was likely to slow down private investment."[21] This view was also expressed by A. Lawrence who noted that "there is no doubt that the events in Indochina or in North Africa led to disaffection towards the possibilities of investment in Black Africa."[22] Thus, it was the entire French colonial empire that was affected. "It is therefore natural that the capitalists should be rather reluctant", wrote Pierre Moussa, evoking "political fears, caused by the events of North Africa and reinforced by the incidents of Suez; one fears that the capital invested in Africa could be neutralized by these problems, or affected by nationalization or appropriation."[23]

In Cameroon, more than elsewhere in the French territories of Black Africa, the growth of nationalism explains the reluctance of private investors in the 1950s. The program of the UPC, from its birth in 1948, had promoted independence and unification with the British Cameroons. In 1951, the emphasis shifted to the question of the non-negotiable movement towards independence. Rumors of independence or autonomy that other political movements also began to demand, were more and more often heard. A glimpse of the position of the French Government can be ascertained from the following statement made by Louis Jacquinot, Minister of Overseas France, in 1954 during a meeting with the leaders of the traditional association of the Duala people known as Ngondo:

> France is trying to grant the territory, as quickly as possible and during the course of its development, all the institutions that will enable it to attain the independence to which the trusteeship agreement shall lead.[24]

The above words could be interpreted as an implicit recognition by the French Government of the right of Cameroon to independence. Louis Jacquinot's declaration contributed to fanning the rumors of independence or autonomy the consequences of which for private investors were inevitable in the eyes of observers:

> The more these rumors, these declarations, these demands are heard the more doubtful the chances are for Cameroon developing through significant investments, through an industrialization which presupposes billions in investment.
>
> The caution of metropolitan financing groups is known, and neither will foreign capital take risks without solid guarantees, especially in overseas territories that are still in their infancy.
>
> However, all these rumors of independence—this nationalism which is rising and becoming increasingly urgent and intransigent—leaves room to suppose that France will leave Cameroon within ten years, or perhaps even sooner.
>
> This is indeed the question. For the moment, and for another year or two, the request will be made tactfully. But who can say that in another two or three years the French Administration won't simply be asked to leave?
>
> The moment for making all this noise could not be more inopportune. Without being a prophet of doom, it can be predicted that in a year from now, the political movements of Cameroon will make such a tam-tam with the word "independence" that Cameroon will be totally blacklisted by French as well as foreign capital.[25]

The above-cited prediction proved to be quite right. Between January and May 1955, several political movements allied to the Administration adopted some of the demands of the UPC, such as political autonomy or even the right of Cameroonians to decide about their belonging to the French Union. All the objectives for which the nationalist party had fought were henceforth officially considered sound and reasonable. The *Proclamation commune* ("Joint Proclamation") of April 22, 1955, which demanded the end of the trusteeship and the establishment of a sovereign state in Cameroon was also evoked. Indeed this was what triggered the riots of May 1955. The growth of nationalism in Cameroon and elsewhere in the French Union explains the mad rush to desert the overseas territories which overtook metropolitan investors in the mid-1950s. *Le Cameroun Libre,* basing itself on analyses of the Parisian press and on numerous testimonies, made it clear that in France, indeed, the financiers no longer wanted to hear about investments in the French overseas territories:

> There is a surplus of French capital to be invested…it begs to be invested.
> But those who have it do not wish to hear about the French overseas territories. They will invest their money anywhere, in South America, in New Zealand, or even in Greenland, but not in French Africa, unless they are given credible and solid guaranties.
> Their caution has psychological and political reasons.…The series of desertions, by France,…in Indochina, in the Caribbean, in Fezzan, her loss of influence in Tunisia, in Morocco, the events of Algeria, all make them doubt the political stability of the territories which belong to the French Union.
> The Cameroonians will never realize the enormous harm that has been done to their country, concerning French and foreign investment, by the climate of political unrest and demands for autonomy, which have been expressed forcefully for two or three years. It has often been said that nothing is easier to alarm than capital. In Cameroon all was done, by the Cameroonians themselves, to keep those who could have taken a risk at arm's length, and even to chase away those who were already established there.[26]

A few months later, the same newspaper, always mindful of the evolution of the question, noted that metropolitan investors no longer showed any interest in Cameroon, because of the political agitation that ravaged the territory. This remark was as follows:

> For a long time, apart from the question of aluminum, we do not recall any visit made to the territory by high profile personalities from economic circles, by businessmen, by representatives of French institutions, for the purpose of seeing "what could be done in Cameroon."
> Somewhat as Marshall Tito who, recently in Moscow, bypassed the Mausoleum of Stalin without stopping, on his way to bow before the tomb of Lenin, Cameroon is bypassed.
> And this is very disturbing.
> It seems, that from the point of view of capital investment, Cameroon has become a country to be struck off the list, with the stroke of a blue pencil.
> The political agitation is the reason for this.

> Certainly, a high-ranking French delegation will not come to see if they could invest a few billions in a territory where the departure of France is evoked in speeches in front of millions of shouting and stomping people.[27]

The case of Cameroon was not unique. The apparent wish to end the colonial system manifested in several French colonies provoked lively reactions in colonial circles, which seemed to some to be attempted blackmail. It was thus, that an inquiry on Africa, written by Raymond Cartier of *Paris-Match*, was presented by Raymond Barbé as a veritable threat, whose crux he summarized this way: "Unless you stay calm, you won't have our money."[28] There was no doubt that the French investors, especially large finance capital, demanded guarantees that would enable them to adapt to an outcome which they felt was inevitable.

As if to demonstrate that they had understood perfectly, Cameroonian political leaders started to make statements to reassure the French. During an interview made in the *maquis* (resistance) in Cameroon on November 21, 1956 by R. Mauriès for *La Dépêche du Midi*, Um Nyobè declared that there was a possibility of Cameroon accepting a system of preferential trade in the future with France, and that he saw the development of Cameroon in collaboration with France and the French, if they wished so. He also recalled that he had always maintained that "we have never confused, we do not confuse and we will not confuse the people of France, our allies, with the French colonialists, our oppressors.[29] Deputy André-Marie Mbida of the French National Assembly, for his part, stated to *Agence France Presse* that the French living in Cameroon will have their place in the new Cameroonian community, they should not be anxious, and will benefit from serious guaranties.[30] In a press conference, Paul Soppo Priso, member of the French Union, president of the ATCAM and a businessman, also wished to reassure the French of Cameroon:

> The word independence, a magic word, to use R. Cartier's phrase, should not scare all the French, and especially not those who are established here, and should not present a barrier to investment, which Cameroon will always be in need of.
>
> Independence will not under any circumstances mean a rupture for a country such as Cameroon whose spirit and soul were "shaped" in a way by France.…Even if some Cameroonians simplistically think that the independence of Cameroon means total isolation and the departure of the French, they will definitely not be followed by their compatriots in this belief.
>
> As it is impossible to imagine that Cameroon would break with France on either the spiritual or the material plane, the French who are here should calm down.
>
> I even assume that the day our independence will be acknowledged and that as a result confidence and spiritual calm will be restored, Cameroon will freely call upon the support of France, for the edification of a Cameroon where everyone will be able to live and work freely with dignity and for the interest of all.[31]

Soppo Priso also made his position on economic and financial questions clear when he declared:

> We are aspiring to independence, but we intend to remain in the franc zone and to retain close economic and cultural ties with France. By the same token we have no intention, once our status is set, to take steps to limit French investment in Cameroon or to nationalize the existing firms, as some people fear. My friends and I myself know very well that a country like ours cannot live alone, nor even completely independently.[32]

There are other statements of this sort, as well as other kinds of benefits and guarantees to French financial groups, that were decided sometimes by the territory (tax relief and long-term engagement), and sometimes by the French State (contribution to capital formation, loans and subventions, guaranteed interest rates, insurance against political risks).

The majority of the causes presented here to explain private disinvestment in Cameroon during the 1950s had been evoked already in 1951 as factors that could determine the behavior of private investment in Cameroon. The following can be read in the Blin Report:

> Some think that the metropolitan currency is bound to be devalued and that of Cameroon will not follow. This is what gives rise to the idea of transferring funds to Cameroon. It must be acknowledged that this consideration plays some role. In any case, this is likely to bring capital to Cameroon, but not to be invested there.
> For capital outside of Cameroon much more powerful is the contrary case: the fear or expectation of a devaluation of the CFA Franc. What is more, if this fear were to disappear, the fact that the buying power of the CFA Franc is slightly lower than that of the Metropolitan Franc prevents a great deal of liquid assets from staying in Cameroon.[33]
> [On stability and political security] Some concede that the invasion of France is inevitable, and feel that it is necessary to turn toward Africa. As a result the steps taken by some companies seem like evacuations....
> Some companies think that, in the event of war, a territory with an international status could offer them a valuable operations field....
> Others think that it is precisely this status which will bring Cameroon to distance itself from France and that a "self-government" (the experiment has just been made in Indochina, despite all denials) will have to thrust aside French companies. Hence, some are loathe to invest, and some admit to maximizing profits while it is still possible and to transferring them immediately as soon as they are realized....
> Thus the same idea brings different companies to act differently.[34]

The combination of all these factors and the conjuncture of financial and political causes explain private disinvestment in Cameroon during the 1950s. *Le Cameroun Libre* summarized this viewpoint rather well:

> Among the causes of the slowing down of private investment, and especially of the influx of fresh capital from the *métropole*, the ravages of a ruinous tax system must definitely be cited in first place.... After that there are the perennial uncertainties surrounding the fate of the CFA Franc, despite the reassurances of the ministers, there is the precedent of the piastre.
> The constant rise in social costs is also a cause for anxiety regarding the placement of capital.
> Finally there are the political incidents. The cases of Indochina and North Africa definitely had repercussions which reached as far as Black Africa. The constant allusions certain political parties of Cameroon make to independence (even if it is to be within the framework of the French Union) are enough to turn both French and foreign capital away from the territory. This is the most obvious consequence of the crusade started since Cameroon's political awakening.[35]

Private disinvestment was not exclusive to Cameroon. It affected the entire French colonial empire starting in 1951. It is difficult to say whether it was more significant in Cameroon than elsewhere. By contrast, it is clear that concerning private investment in French Black Africa, Cameroon constituted a privileged field. "The comparison with French West Africa shows a greater and more sustained development of private investment. While the influx of capital in 1952 was only three times that of 1947 in French West Africa, it was seven times greater in Cameroon."[36] According to the statistics of the Ministry of Overseas France, in 1949 there were 450 new companies and companies increasing their capital in French Black Africa (French Equatorial Africa, French West Africa, Togo and Cameroon), of which 62 (13.7 percent) were in Cameroon; in the same year the total amount of the capital investment was 3,739.6 million CFA Francs, of which 369.2 (9.8 percent) was in Cameroon. In 1952, these numbers rose to 462 companies of which 136 (29.4 percent) were in Cameroon and to 5,844.4 million CFA Francs, of which 1,469 (25.13 percent) were in Cameroon.[37] In 1953, 26.2 percent of these companies and 21.2 percent of the capital were still in the territory.

The privileged status of Cameroon in the field of French public investment overseas from 1946 to 1956 has been demonstrated earlier. The above figures make it possible to state that this territory was also a privileged region for French private investment in Black Africa.

NOTES

1. *Le Cameroun Libre*, 488 (February 1–15, 1955): 1.
2. In general many companies were driven to court-supervised liquidation or bankruptcy,

especially after 1953. For examples, see *Marchés Coloniaux*, especially 413, 515, 518, 529, 549. In a speech made on October 21, 1955 on the occasion of the opening of the budgetary session of ATCAM, the High Commissioner, Roland Pré, acknowledged that there were in Cameroon "bankruptcies and the closing of businesses especially in the sector of small and medium size enterprises" (*Archives de l'Institut Charles de Gaulle*—AICDG—61).

3. "Faut-il ou non pousser l'industrialisation ?" *Le Cameroun Libre*, 516 (January 1–15, 1956): 2.
4. *Marchés Coloniaux*, 485 (February 26, 1955): 613.
5. "Après le scandale des piastres, le scandale des francs CFA," *Le Cameroun Libre* (December 1–15, 1953): 2.
6. *Marchés Coloniaux*, 481 (January 29, 1955): 381.
7. *JORF, débats de l'Assemblée de l'Union Française* (1947–1948, session of January 30, 1948): 28.
8. Cited in *Bulletin d'Information de la France d'Outre Mer*, 120 (May 15, 1948): 8.
9. *Le Cameroun Libre*, 374 (May 15, 1950): 2.
10. *Le Cameroun Libre*, 377 (July 15, 1950): 2.
11. *Marchés Coloniaux*, 480 (January 22, 1955): 179.
12. *Le Cameroun Libre*, 459 (November 15–30, 1953).
13. "Le problème du franc CFA," *Climats*, 185 (July 1, 1949): 5.
14. "La politique de M. Robert Buron outre mer," *Climats*, 460 (October 14–20, 1954): 3.
15. Lawrence (A.), "Les investissements dans les territoires d'outre mer," *JORF, Conseil économique, avis et rapports* (March 7, 1956): 122.
16. Cited in "La fiscalité écrasante des territoires d'outre mer," *Le Cameroun Libre*, 465 (February 1954): 3.
17. Ngayewang (P.), "Opinion camerounaise. Important malaise économique," *La Presse du Cameroun* (February 24, 1954): 1.
18. "Les dépenses du personnel sont un gouffre sans fonds," *Le Cameroun Libre*, 481 (October 15–31, 1954): 1-2.
19. "L'administration freine-t-elle l'économie du Cameroun?" *La Presse du Cameroun* (July 1955); and *Marchés Coloniaux*, 505 (July 16, 1955): 2029.
20. "Investissement en Afrique," *Le Cameroun Libre*, 509 (December 15–31, 1955): 2.
21. Durand (H.), *Essai sur la conjoncture de l'Afrique noire* (Paris: Dalloz, 1957), p. 77.
22. *JORF, Conseil Economique* (January 12, 1957).
23. Moussa (P.), p. 158.
24. Cited in *Le Cameroun Libre*, 473 (June 15-30, 1954): 1.
25. "Les conséquences inéluctables d'une poussée du nationalisme," *Le Cameroun Libre*, *Ibid.*
26. "Investissements en Afrique," *Le Cameroun Libre*, 509 (December 15–31, 1955): 1.
27. "On ne s'arrête plus au Cameroun," *Le Cameroun Libre*, 522 (July 1–15, 1956): 2.
28. Barbé (R.), "Quelques données économiques sur la crise du système colonial français," *Economie et Politique* (July 1957): 23.
29. *La Dépêche du Midi* (December 8, 1956). See also Um Nyobè (R.), p. 391.
30. "La voix des hommes raisonnables," *Le Cameroun Libre*, 528 (October 1–15, 1956): 1.
31. "La conférence de presse de Paul Soppo Priso," *L'Effort Camerounais* (October 28 - November 30, 1956): 1.
32. *Le Cameroun Libre*, 530 (November 1–15, 1956).
33. By way of example it should be mentioned that in 1950, 892 million CFA Francs were transferred from France by postal money orders, as opposed to 76 million in the opposite direction. As for bank transfers, the figures are as follows: Cameroon-France, 3,636 million;

France-Cameroon, 2,069 million. During the first third of 1951, bank transfers were 1,074 million in the direction of Cameroon-France and 300 million in the opposite direction, whereas money orders amounted to 280 million against 31 million (ANSOM, affaires économiques 84–85, Rapport Blin, 1951).

34. ANSOM, affaires économiques 84–85, *Ibid.*
35. "Les investissements privés se font rares en Afrique," *Le Cameroun Libre*, 489 (February 15–28, 1955).
36. Didier (H.), p. 153.
37. *Documents Statistiques du Ministère de la France d'Outre Mer*, 12.

Chapter 8

The Financial and Social Impact of FIDES Investment

The FIDES Program: an Unprofitable and False Gift

The effects of the FIDES loans invested in Cameroon were the modernization of old infrastructure, the creation of new infrastructure, and the provision of production facilities. But in return, the territorial budget had to pay personnel expenses, materials and maintenance resulting from these additional investments. In the minds of the directors of FIDES, meeting this obligation was not supposed to cause any special financial difficulties for the territory. It was admitted that the execution of the First Four-Year Plan, which was almost exclusively dedicated to infrastructural projects, would bring to local finances increased costs that would be difficult to shoulder since the economic level of the country was still low. The Second Plan, that was more oriented towards the expansion of cash crops, would allow the Cameroonian budget to offset the losses by an increase in customs duties deriving from increased exports.

The evolution of the financial situation of Cameroon contradicted these optimistic forecasts. The growth in investment was not followed by a corresponding growth in revenues. In Cameroon the relationship between the economy and finance was particularly direct, because the bulk of the resources came from export duties. However, by the end of the Second Four-Year Plan, this investment policy had not yet increased cash crop production sufficiently to offset the additional operating costs to which it gave rise. During the execution of the first two four-year plans, most of the FIDES loans were indeed dedicated to the development of the infrastructure. This orientation was deemed necessary for an underdeveloped country which lacked modern means of communication, but it had no direct impact whatsoever on the level of production. Equipment projects directly linked to production were not undertaken until about 1953 when rural modernization sectors were created. But, investments of this nature could increase the marketable quantities significantly only after a minimum period of four or five years; thus, their full effects were to be felt only by 1960. Secondly, from 1951 on the financial situation of Cameroon was characterized by growing budget deficits.

It became clear that the implementation of FIDES projects was the cause of the excess spending in relation to revenue and that the Plan was not only a "false gift" which led to operating costs that the budget could not offset, but also an unprofitable enterprise.[1] In an internship report to the *Ecole Nationale d'Administration* (ENA—National School of Administration, France) in 1957, R. Richard evoked Cameroonian public opinion on that subject:

> Public opinion in Cameroon noted certain connections between the improvement of equipment and the aggravation of the financial situation. It also denounces the lack of economic and financial productivity of the investments and thus has no trouble in deploring the rigidity of the FIDES doctrine, which imposes all of the operating costs resulting from economic and social progress on the territory.[2]

There is a connection between the implementation of FIDES loans and the onset of the financial problems of Cameroon. The activities of the Plan officially began in 1947, a year of balanced budget for the territory. But, according to R. Richard, only 7 percent of the loans of the First Four-Year Plan, representing the initial costs of the installation of firms, were paid by June 30, 1949. Thus the first equipment projects began to weigh on the territorial budget during the fiscal years of 1950 or 1951. Indeed, it was in the closing accounts of these years that the phenomenon of the budget deficit appeared in Cameroon for the first time.

Table 8.1

The growth of the number of civil servants by sector in Cameroon from 1947 to 1955

	1947	1950	1955
Social services	1,801	1,865	6,797
Public works domain	396	563	2,280
Economic services	485	518	1,697

Source: Adapted from R. Richard, p. 4.

Similarly, 1951 constituted a key transitional year in terms of the composition of the public service sector. In this sector, the growth of personnel that was steady until then, suddenly started to develop faster. According to R. Richard, the general increase from 1947 to 1950 was barely more than 2,000 employees whereas from 1950 to 1953 it was 5,500 and from 1953 to 1955 it reached 6,500. The increase was especially important in the sectors in which FIDES invested. Table 8.1 shows this increase. It was generally thought that given the magnitude of the capital effort the budget deficits and the growth in the number of civil servants constituted two inevitable phenomena.

The Financial Costs of FIDES Investment

By June 30, 1956 FIDES had spent or pledged to spend 26 billion CFA Francs on Cameroon. Compared to the territorial budget, that was 3 billion in 1949 and 10 billion in 1956, this sum represents eight and two and a half times the budget for these fiscal years respectively. If we accept along with R. Richard the conclusions of a study by André Postel-Vinay, Director of CCFOM, who calculated the relationship between the operating costs and the value of corresponding investments at approximately 11 percent, the charges that weighed on Cameroon as a consequence of the activities of FIDES were at minimum nearly 4 billion, which represented more than one third of the territorial budget of 1956.[3] It is possible that the above-defined mathematical relationship, which should not be seen as an absolute value, was higher than the actual cost. Nonetheless, it is difficult to imagine that such massive investments did not impose an impossible weight on the territorial budget. Even if these opinions seem exaggerated, it is clear that social and economic progress led to new expenditures for which the FIDES plan was in part responsible.

But the responsibility of the Plan should not be overstated, as the French report on this Plan and the development of Cameroon shows. In effect, this report stated that:

> A detailed examination of the costs of FIDES investments and of the results of economic analysis shows that in reality the balance of these actions is positive; that the budget deficit comes from the growth of operational spending, but that the proportion of the Plan in this growth is only 15%.

However, the authors of the report added:

> An additional 300 million should have been allocated annually in order for the investments actually made to become fully profitable, which would have brought the proportion of the Plan in the operational costs to 17.5%.[4]

The French Administration in Cameroon attempted to assess the operating costs of FIDES investment. The figures used stop on June 30, 1956. About this assessment several comments need to be made. Firstly, the method of direct assessment does not necessarily exclude arbitrariness, due to the difficulty of separating the expenses deriving from a new investment and those related to already existing and previously working equipment. The new expenses were only a continuation of the original expenses and it would not be possible to clearly identify the exact cut-off point. The same actors used new and old installations indiscriminately. Secondly, the benefiting services may have had a tendency to minimize the operating expenses deriving from investment loans, because they thought that if the percentage of the former by comparison to the latter were too high, the service of the Plan would reduce investments in the sectors where the operating costs were deemed to be too high.

These remarks do not, however, significantly modify the information provided. The additional cost imposed on the territorial budget was assessed at approximately 588 million CFA Francs regarding annual debt service, and at approximately 965 million with regard to the annual expenses of the operations relating to the infrastructure, rural economy, education and health.[5]

The first of these numbers represents the costs which are the normal counterpart of the loans granted by CCFOM and destined within the framework of the FIDES program to ensure the contribution of the territory to its equipment. Thus the territory was supposed to dedicate more than 5 percent of its budget annually to the reimbursements and interest payment on these loans. There is no doubt that this was a heavy burden. By comparison, the amount of annual spending set aside for the operation of equipment projects seems low. It represents only 10 percent of the budget, and 4 percent of the totality of credit granted to Cameroon by FIDES. These proportions of 10 percent and 4 percent are far from those determined by André Postel-Vinay whose figures generally correspond to those arrived at by public opinion: 30 percent and more than 10 percent respectively.[6]

This relatively weak percentage of expenditure attributable to FIDES in comparison to the total of the operating costs can be explained by several factors. First, there is the insufficiency of budgetary credit for the maintenance of equipment. Secondly, the local French Administration itself was responsible for some of the increased spending: namely the growth in personnel and salaries independent of the implementation of FIDES loans. Finally, the transfer of part of the operating costs to budgets other than the territorial one can be mentioned. Part of the operating costs resulting from the increase in equipment was indeed supported by the French state budget and, in Cameroon either by special or local budgets or by individual beneficiaries themselves. Thus, the French state budget took charge of the bulk of the personnel and maintenance expenses of the aviation infrastructure. In the same way, FIDES underwrote the operations of agricultural modernization sectors on which the development of the rural economy was based.

In Cameroon the financial effort was also partly supported by the beneficiaries of the FIDES investments. For example, the port and railway services supported their own operating expenses. In the field of local administration, communes, regions, and subdivisions were supposed to pay for road maintenance. They were also responsible for the partial payment of expenses related to personnel, for the materials and maintenance of educational and medical establishments from which their members benefited, and for the functioning of projects of a purely local interest (for example communal cocoa dryers, roads, and wells) which were conceptualized and executed within the framework of the so-called "small rural equipment" projects. Finally, Cameroonians themselves paid taxes which were collected to pay for the benefits gained from the introduction of water and electricity in towns and villages.

This significant contribution of local organizations and individuals shows that the territorial budget, faced with a situation which was acknowledged to be "frankly bad", was not alone in shouldering the costs resulting from the financial relations with the *métropole*. A wide cross-section of Cameroonian society bore the costs imposed by the investments of the Plan.

FIDES: a Source of Social Frustration

There is a striking contrast between the economic changes directly resulting from the large-scale investment program in the territory, and the very limited political changes the French were willing to concede. This difference between economic and political change was one the most glaring contradictions in Cameroonian society. The three High-Commissioners of France in Cameroon between 1947 and 1956, René Hoffher, André Soucadaux and Roland Pré, wished—and they insisted on this point—to actively pursue the economic expansion of the territory. They considered politics to be of secondary importance, if not downright harmful, to what they considered to be their most important task.[7] This policy was strongly criticized by Cameroonian nationalists. Here is, for example, the statement made by Ruben Um Nyobè concerning that matter:

> For years we have been demanding the participation of Cameroonians in the management of the affairs of their country through the mediation of the representative, legislative and executive organs; this demand is in keeping with the principles of the International Trusteeship System and with the often repeated wishes of the General Assembly of the United Nations. Not only does the French Government disregard

> completely these aspirations and the recommendations of the UNO on this question, but the French colonialists try to derail the debate by opposing our political demands with the preposterous slogan of "economic and social projects," while these famous projects rather than becoming the national patrimony of tomorrow serve to profit only the colonialists who shamelessly exploit the people and the wealth of Cameroon.[8]

The labor demands engendered by the economic programs of the Plan quickly drew a great number of Cameroonians to the new sectors of activity, but their role and that of their political representatives in determining the economic priorities of the country remained extremely limited. "Indeed, they always managed to make and execute the plans without the actual support of the indigenous population. The powers of the Assembly were laughable; in all questions they were limited to the expression of their views, which meant that the point of view of the Board of Directors of FIDES, that is to say of the Ministry of Overseas France, always prevailed in the end."[9] To illustrate the above point, it is worth quoting at length the statement made in 1957 by Charles Okala, a Cameroonian political leader, during one of the sessions of ATCAM:

> To say that we had been closely associated with the elaboration of the plans is a half-truth; I will give the example of *Route Razel*: can it be said that this Assembly approved this road? Well, the docket had been rejected, and five times the Government sent it back to us, because the *métropole* did not wish to release the funds to maintain the already existing road network. They wished to create a prestige road. Can it be said that the Assembly accepted the creation of *Route Razel* with a happy heart? I say no, and as long as the *métropole* was not satisfied, we did not wish to build this road.
>
> As for the Yabassi-Ndiki road, whether it was the early or the latest Representative Assembly we always voted on motions…to include it in the plan; as long as the Plan did not get what it wanted, this question was always sent back to us, and just until now nothing had been done. Thus it cannot be said that the Assembly was closely linked to this plan, because this plan was not conceived in Paris and it did not have the approval of certain pontiffs who, wish to regulate the projects which should be carried out in Cameroon from Paris.…
>
> As for the water works of Mokolo…until now the Plan did not wish to grant significant loans. There is a study carried out by the Public Works Department which concluded that a dam could be constructed on the Ndi in order to provide Mokolo with water in all seasons. Because this project was not accepted in Paris, nothing had been done.
>
> Whereas [ATCAM] had several times voted in a diametrically opposed sense, the Administration had renewed its attack.…When the Administration was not pleased the vote was not taken into consideration. With regard to the Plan, the Assembly only ratifies. It had no initiative. This is what had to be said today, and this is what everyone should know.[10]

During the same session another member of the ATCAM, Jean Ekwabi, underlined the powerlessness of the local assembly in determining the direction the economic programs of Cameroon should take when he made the following statement:

> ...ATCAM found itself faced with a veto, which did not allow it to introduce any modifications to the note which was to be presented by the French Administration, after it had been studied superficially by the Assembly and submitted to the vote of this Assembly.

The paradoxical situation evoked here had the consequence of increasing frustration and bitterness among many Cameroonians who were powerless to counter what in their eyes was the misuse of the human and financial resources of the country. In order to understand these feelings, it is necessary to see how the loans of the FIDES program were used in Cameroon.

FIDES Achievements

By the end of the decade that followed the Second World War, FIDES achievements could be found in various sectors in Cameroon. In the area of the rural economy, the implementation from 1947 to 1956 of a rural infrastructure manifested itself in the creation, equipment and operation of numerous technical installations including the Agricultural Research Center of Nkolbisson; the production station of Nkoemvoné; the Rice station of Logone; the disinfection center of Douala; the production and animal reproduction center of Kouden and Wakwa; the reforestation centers of Baleng and Melap in the West, and the registry offices of the dense forest at Bonépoupa, Kribi and Mbalmayo.

Table 8.2 and figure 8.1 contain the data that makes it possible to review the development of the principal Cameroonian export products from 1946 to 1956. The volume of some of these products, especially coffee, peanuts and cotton, appears to be rising fairly constantly from 1946 to 1956, while other products, such as cocoa and banana, experienced an appreciable variation in their volume from year to year, and the export of palm oil saw a net weakening from 1949 to 1956.

The development of these exports depended heavily on production itself. In this context, it should be noted that in a general sense during the decade following the Second World War, the production as well as the export of agricultural cash crops rose sharply in Cameroon. There are several explanations for this phenomenon. In the case of cocoa, for example, the growth in the production of this agricultural raw material was a consequence of the efforts made by the French not only to develop the territory, but also to create a *classe conservatrice* (conservative class), by helping to bring about prosperity in the rural areas in order to moderate the ardor of anti-colonial demands, and to reinforce the predisposition of certain cocoa planters to collaborate with their

Table 8.2

Principal exports of Cameroon from 1946 to 1956 (Q: quantity in tons; V: value in millions of CFA Francs)

	Cocoa		Peanuts		Cotton		Palm Oil	
	Q	V	Q	V	Q	V	Q	V
1946	35,488	362.2	1,683	3.1	223	2.2	1,552	9.0
1947	33,701	626.1	1,989	15.9	83	0.9	1,023	13.3
1948	47,916	1,942.2	2,432	49.4	183	1.9	2,352	66.3
1949	48,014	3,177.6	4,070	12.3	115	2.2	6,281	256.7
1950	43,722	3,977.0	4,894	115.1	41	1.3	4,740	201.8
1951	48,805	5,841.6	5,905	165.9	85	7.8	4,579	190.9
1952	51,089	5,961.8	8,454	264.6	295	36.4	2,123	53.7
1953	60,489	7,111.6	4,758	53.1	1,299	160.3	770	13.7
1954	50,032	8,276.9	8,968	287.0	2,060	295.0	724	14.7
1955	55,587	8,128.2	7,930	286.4	4,071	585.2	457	2.7
1956	45,965	4,541.3	8,971	320.8	5,235	725.9	745	27.7

	Coffee		Bananas		Timber	
	Q	V	V	Q	Q	V
1946	5,858	117.0	59.7	1,683	36,710	101.9
1947	5,561	168.5	240.1	1,989	32,424	95.3
1948	7,265	297.1	797.8	2,432	63,221	238.1
1949	8,187	690.7	1,005.8	4,070	61,760	259.0
1950	7,653	1,082.5	1,011.5	4,894	68,869	332.0
1951	8,682	1,496.9	1,008.3	5,905	64,097	417.9
1952	9,241	1,636.8	955.9	8,454	41,795	296.7
1953	9,614	1,836.5	1,168.9	4,758	46,266	284.8
1954	11,372	2,395.2	1,186.6	8,968	57,007	336.1
1955	13,909	3,767.7	1,229.3	7,930	70,020	445.7
1956	17,793	2,652.8	1,063.8	8,971	79,331	513.4

Source: "Commerce extérieur du Cameroun oriental."

Figure 8.1

Development of the quantity of the principal exports of Cameroon from 1946 to 1956

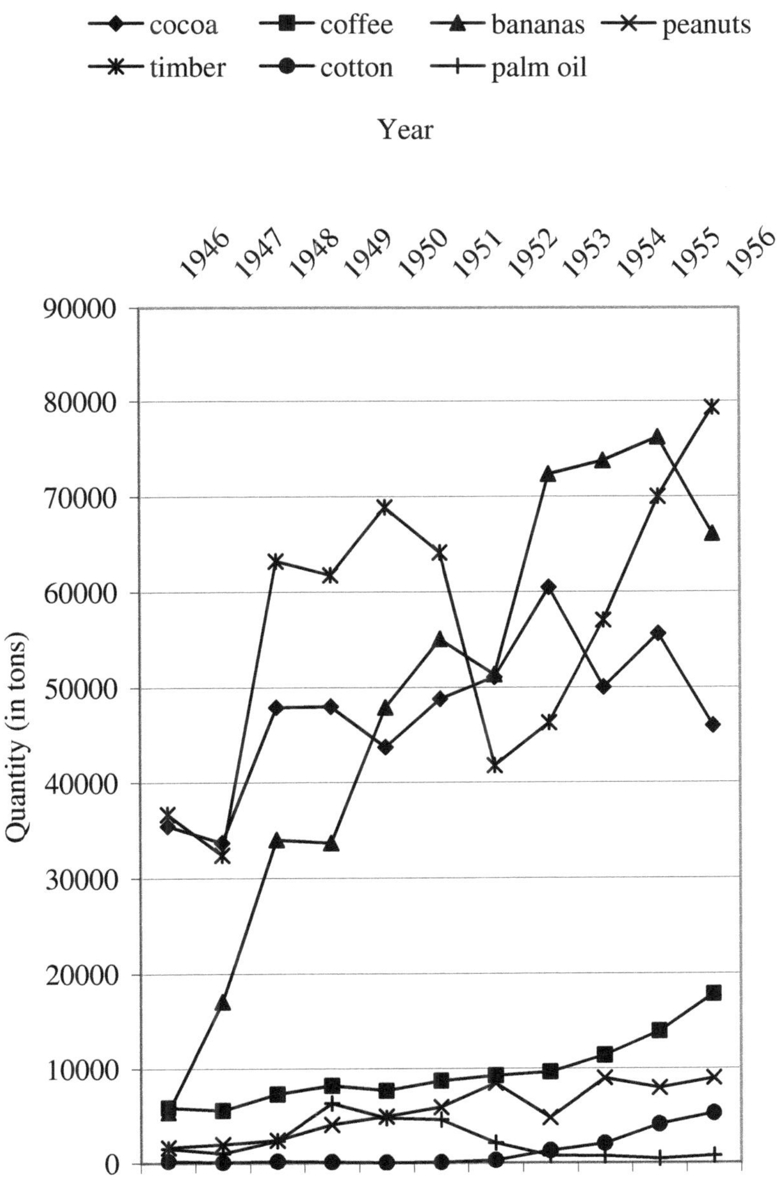

colonial masters. At the end of the Second World War, and prior to the drop in the export price of cocoa some twelve years later, the stable incomes brought by this crop resulted politically in a very moderate and even optimistic attitude. By contrast, the end of the economic boom and the fall in prices, starting in 1955, led to the growth of anti-colonialism in the cocoa growing regions.

The increase in the tonnage of timber could first be explained by the technical improvements made in forestry exploitation. However, this technical progress had its negative side: it seemed to the inhabitants to be going against their growing need for available employment. The most important among them were the inhabitants of the Sanaga Maritime, inasmuch as this region had the largest number of companies working in forestry. This sector owed its importance in the Sanaga Maritime to the combined presence of forests and the railways. After agriculture and public works, forestry employed the largest number of manual laborers in the territory, and this is the other factor which explains the rise in the production and in the export of Cameroonian timber from 1946 to 1956.

If the tonnage of cocoa, coffee, banana, timber, peanuts and cotton increased in a satisfactory way, the opposite can be said of palm kernel and palm oil production. Under the Germans both represented the second most important export products after rubber. During the 1950s, their commercial quantity stagnated or regressed. The bulk of these two agricultural products was neither put on the market nor exported. This decline is one of the main explanations for the impoverishment of the Bassaà area, where palm nut and palm oil were the main agricultural products. The problems resulting from forestry exploitation and agricultural production in the Bassaà area made this region the potential reservoir of revolutionary nationalism in Cameroon.

To continue with the balance sheet of the Plan, it must be noted that there were some failures or semi-failures in production itself, such as the attempt to launch the mechanized production of peanuts in the north of Cameroon, the creation of quinquina plantations in Dschang and the construction of a quinine extraction plant.

In the infrastructural field, one of the most noteworthy projects was the hydro-electric plant of Edéa which led to the establishment of ALUCAM-Péchiney-Ugine. The total of classified roads grew from less than 4,000 km in 1948 to 6,416 km in 1956, of which 577 km were asphalted, and to which we should add 4,000 km of non-classified roads. Many bridges were constructed over the Wouri River (1,800 meters long); the Lom River at Ayos; at Kikot; on the Ngaoundéré-Maroua road; on the Bafang road; and on the Kribi-Edéa, Kribi-Lolodorf, and the Bafia-Eséka road. Yaoundé, Douala, Nkongsamba and Edéa had waterworks constructed. The electrification of Douala, Yaoundé, Nkongsamba, Edéa, Garoua, Maroua and Dschang also took place. The capacity of the port of Douala which was 20,000 tons at the beginning of the Plan was enlarged to handle 767,000 tons in 1957, and that of the Garoua port rose from 25,000 tons in 1947 to 40,000 tons in 1955. The railway system was modernized and as a result the amount of goods transported grew from 250,000 tons in 1947 to 650,000 tons in 1957. The improvement of the runways of the main airfields of the territory besides that of Douala (Yaoundé, Ngaoundéré, Garoua, and Maroua) made possible a considerable and sustained development of commercial air transportation. The total traffic of these four airfields increased from 1,245 planes in 1950 to more than 9,000 by 1950; the number of passengers grew from 7,950 in 1950 to more than 36,000 in 1955, and the tonnage of freight rose from 300 tons in 1950 to more than 5,000 tons in 1955.

In the social field, health and education were the areas that were the most affected by the FIDES investments. In 1957, Cameroon had 314 dispensaries of which 243 were public institutions, that is to say one dispensary for 10,000 inhabitants. During the preceding years 41 hospital buildings and ten maternity wards were constructed. The main medical centers, including the hospitals of Douala and Yaoundé, were enlarged and modernized and the important medical research center of Yaoundé got new equipment. From 1947 to 1955, the number of hospitalized patients, of hospitalization days, of consultations, and of consultants increased respectively from 32,872 to 73,236, from 890,044 to 1,696,885, from 3,915,570 to 7,821,939, and from 1,227,549 to 2,575,512. An infrastructure was put in place for the prevention and treatment of some contagious illnesses including leprosy, treponematoses, tuberculosis, malaria, and sleeping sickness.

With regard to education, Cameroon had 2,465 schools in 1957, including 583 public primary schools, 1,787 private primary schools, 18 public secondary schools, 35 private secondary schools, and 70 educational centers. There were 278,907 students including 59,856 boys and 23,618 girls in the public schools, and 198,798 boys and 52,636 girls in the private schools. From 1952 to 1957, the percentage of the population in school, excluding the Northern regions, rose from 39 to 74 percent. Furthermore the number of holders of various certificates of general education (CEPE, BE, BEPC) grew from 100 to 240 during the same period, and the number of high school graduates increased from 1 in 1948 to 452 in 1956.[11]

It was within the framework of the two four-year plans that the above-enumerated projects and accomplishments were achieved. During the First Four-Year Plan the officials of the Ministry of Overseas France and the colonial administration of Cameroon had decided to emphasize the infrastructural development of the territory. To a great extent, they focused on major projects, such as the modernization and extension of the port of Douala, the construction of a magnificent bridge on the Wouri River at Douala completed with a railway line, the improvement of the road network, especially between Douala and its hinterland, and the renovation of the railway system. Clearly, the majority of these undertakings concerned Douala.

Although the Second Plan anticipated more direct social measures affecting the welfare of the Cameroonian people, the First Plan had a greater social impact, structuring the Cameroonian economy in such a particular way that attempts to correct this disequilibrium during the Second Plan remained ineffective and superficial. The data in table 8.3 serve to further illustrate this subject. This table and figure 8.2 show the distribution of FIDES loans in Cameroon by sectors and periods.

The distribution of the FIDES loans in Cameroon was unequal. First, the amount spent during the First Four-Year Plan was almost double that of the Second Plan: out of a total of approximately 28 billion CFA Francs spent from 1946 to 1956, the amount invested during the First Four-Year Plan was about 18 billion, as opposed to about 10 billion during the Second Four-Year Plan. Secondly and significantly, FIDES basically invested in the infrastructural sector. Cameroonian criticisms of the FIDES program as it was carried out in Cameroon considered the overemphasis on infrastructural development to be one of its main shortcomings. A French commentator who took the opposite view, that is to say that in all French territories the great majority of the loans of the First Four-Year Plan were devoted to infrastructure was nonetheless forced to conclude that this proportion was 75 percent in Cameroon, as opposed to 50 percent in West Africa.[12] Statistics show that the portion utilized for infrastructure even exceeded 75 percent during the first plan: the figure that

Table 8.3

Distribution by economic sectors and periods of FIDES loans in Cameroon (in CFA Francs)

	First Plan	Second Plan	TOTAL
Rural economy	758,750,000	3,875,500,000	4,634,250,000
Infrastructure (transport and communication)	15,741,714,245	4,745,000,000	20,481,714,245
Social equipment	1,762,400,000	2,029,000,000	3,791,400,000

Source: *ATCAM, Journal des débats*, séance du 27 avril 1957, p. 498.

Figure 8.2

Distribution by economic sectors and by periods of the FIDES loans in Cameroon

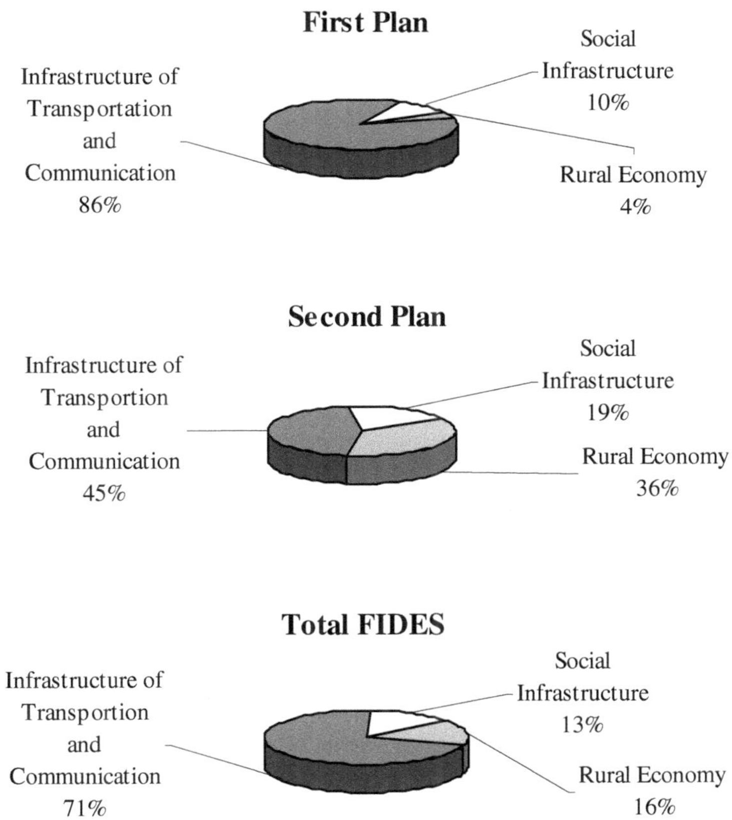

was given by the French Administration is actually 85 percent.[13] A calculation made using the figures from table 8.3 produces practically the same percentage. The same calculation also shows that more than 70 percent of the total FIDES loans from 1947 to 1956 were infrastructural investments.

One could ask whether in a country which needed primarily to produce enough to feed its inhabitants such a massive infrastructural investment program was not established for reasons of imperial prestige and in order to satisfy special interests rather than to promote the well-being of the Cameroonian peasants. Here is the answer of someone who should know, Dr. Louis Paul Aujoulat:

> There was indeed an element of capitalist greed in the Plan on behalf of enterprises which thought that the Plan had been made for them and for their benefit; and indeed, we saw shocking things: a bridge constructed on a Cameroonian river in an area where there was no road, and this bridge was built nonetheless; the material arrived by way of paths through the forest; and when the bridge was completed, one asked oneself what to do with it....Naturally, roads had to be built so that nonetheless this bridge could eventually be good for something. I could also evoke a magnificent hospital built in an area where there were no patients because there were no people. I could alas multiply similar examples which would prove that when we talk of capitalist greed in connection with an investment fund for economic and social development in Africa, this is not a fantasy.[14]

The Second Four-Year Plan which was implemented from 1953–1954 emphasized the development of the rural economy. In general, it paid more attention to the social aspects of development, and when it envisioned the improvement of infrastructure, this often consisted of more modest projects concerning roads, schools and health facilities in rural areas. Many of the projects undertaken during the Second Plan were carried out through the channel of the *Société Indigène de Prévoyance* (SIP) and other cooperatives created by the Government. There was a willingness on the part of the planners of 1953–57 to involve Cameroonians in the development of the territory. But in what way? Once again, here is the testimony of Dr. Aujoulat:

> Indeed a number of interesting initiatives constituting an ensemble came into existence. Rural modernization sectors were created. Cooperatives related to traditional mutual help associations were put in place, rural communes were instituted with a view to connect people of the countryside at the grassroots to the management of their immediate affairs. The village communities were designed, so that they would help Cameroonian peasants and ensure that the improvement of their living standards and their conditions really be made with them and for them. And finally after very interesting educational experiments, we arrived at the establishment of a leadership school to educate rural leaders, that is to say young peasants who were to receive a relatively broad preliminary training, who subsequently would return to their villages, where they were to be leaders not only on the level of production but also as human beings. The cooperatives themselves were conceived not only to improve productivity and the conditions of production, but also to take charge of the life of the village at the same time.
> What is more, at the same time Cameroon also innovated on the social level by establishing a fund for social solidarity which was funded by annual contributions and whose leadership was left in the hands of the rural communes to ensure their health and educational development. In the institutional area all the necessary elements were there to attain a very real development.[15]

Thus institutions were brought into existence. Unfortunately it must be said that all kinds of obstacles were put in the way of these institutions as Ajoulat added in his testimony:

> As for rural modernization, it was carried out practically by civil servants...coming from Europe who led the peasant centers for several years and who were thus engaged in improving or organizing production but who were truly cut off from the African peasantry, and with this idea of definitively bringing about the agricultural prosperity of the country in a way that left the Black peasant out.
>
> As for the cooperatives they had been cleverly torpedoed by those who had no interest in seeing cocoa or any other production cooperatives be put in direct touch with factories which were likely to use their product in Europe or elsewhere.
>
> The funds for social solidarity were...absorbed and lost in the general budget. The school for rural leaders was torpedoed because it was seen as a training ground for political militants likely to disturb the Administration.
>
> The rural communes increased in number, but the lectures that we could organize to provide civic education to these councilmen were stopped by order of the administration which saw political intentions in them too.

The fears of the French were well-founded because of the orientation given to the law of April 30, 1946 in Cameroon. The investments to which this law gave rise created a structural imbalance in the Cameroonian economy which was not only a source of economic frustration for Cameroonians of various social strata, but also an obvious target for the nationalists.

NOTES

1. ANSOM, FIDES 351, "Le Plan et l'évolution du Cameroun, 1947–1956," p. 55. See also Hugon (P.), p. 15.
2. Richard (R.), p. 4.
3. *Ibid.*, p. 5.
4. ANSOM, FIDES 351, "Le Plan et l'évolution du Cameroun 1947–1956," p. 55.
5. *Ibid.*, pp. 62–74.
6. Richard (R), p. 9.
7. Joseph (R.), p. 124.
8. Um Nyobè (R.), p. 309.
9. Eyinga (A.), "Dix années de FIDES au Cameroun (1947–1957)" ENFOM, 66 (1958–59): 21.
10. *ATCAM. Journal des débats*. Session budgétaire mars 1957. T1. Séance du 25 mars 1957 au 1er mai 1957. Séance du 27 avril 1957 (Yaoundé: Imprimerie du Gouvernement), p. 519.
11. "Rapport Annuel du Gouvernement Français" (1957), pp. 108–109; *ATCAM, Journal des débats*, séance du 27 avril 1957, pp. 502–503.

12. Didier (H.), p. 153.
13. ANSOM, FIDES 351, "Le Plan et l'évolution du Cameroun, 1947–1956," p. 90.
14. Cited by Eyinga (A.), "Dix années de FIDES," p. 18. One of the principal figures of preindependence politics, Louis Paul Aujoulat was a French medical doctor and a politician who won continous elections into the Cameroon Assembly and the National Assembly in Paris from 1946 to 1956. Between 1949 and 1954 he was Secretary of State for Overseas France, Minister of Health, and Minister of Work and Social Affairs in the Mendès-France Government. Dr. Aujoulat was also cofounder of the Catholic Mission Society *Ad Lucem*, and founder of the political party known as the *Bloc Démocratique Camerounais* (BDC).
15. *Ibid,* p. 22.

Chapter 9

The Economic Impact of FIDES

FIDES and the Structural Imbalance in Cameroon's Economy

Cameroon saw remarkable economic and political development during and immediately after the Second World War mostly due to its strategic importance for the Free French forces. Similarly, the economic importance of Cameroon for the French in the post-war period played a determining role in subsequent political developments. We must think of "the economy" in the broadest sense here, because at least three interconnected aspects need to be taken into account: the economic importance of the territory as a potential source of profits; the geographical significance of Cameroon in comparison with the French territories of Equatorial Africa; and a third factor which reinforces the second, that is the crucial role of the port of Douala for the economic development and exploitation of the entire region. These three aspects were often conflated by observers:

> It is enough to look at a map to understand what is exceptional in the position of Douala—estuary port altogether unique on this coast—neck of an enormous funnel delineated on the African coast between Dakar and the Cape, with all of Central Africa as its natural hinterland.
> It is precisely for this reason that the territories of AEF [French Equatorial Africa], Oubangui-Chari and Chad, find their logical port there....[1]
> Because of its geographical position Douala is the natural outlet, not only for Cameroon, but even for the Gulf of Guinea, Oubangui and Chad. This location justifies its exceptional importance on the West coast of Africa along with Dakar and Abidjan. In addition, Douala is encircled by a zone which is particularly rich in export crops: banana, coffee, cocoa, timber....[2]

During the inter-war period the French often reproached their German predecessors that they had wished to make Cameroon and Douala the basis of a grand *Mittleafrika Kolonie.* But actually they harbored the same idea, albeit on a more modest scale than the Germans. The debate on this question within French colonial circles basically revolved around the question of the railways. The French only extended the lines constructed in Cameroon by the Germans towards Yaoundé by 128 km, and only added a 37 km line from Otélé to Mbalmayo. The line towards the north did not go further than Nkongsamba where the Germans had stopped.

General policy and financial reasons explain why the French did not undertake any railway construction after 1927 in Cameroon and little in their other African territories. In their reports to the UN on Cameroon, the French explained that the rail network had not been developed in Cameroon "because of natural obstacles which would have called for an undertaking out of proportion with the economic imperatives."[3] But the international status of the territory constituted a further political reason which dissuaded them. The French were faced with two choices: the first was to extend the rail network towards the interior, which would only have been desirable if it could have been extended as far as Chad. The particular international status of Cameroon rendered such an investment too risky: it only made sense if Cameroon could be assimilated into the Equatorial colonial empire of France. The reactions of the French to Cameroonian demands for independence and autonomy during the 1950s are easy to imagine; this attitude was indeed deeply felt by the *colons* (settlers) of the territory when they warned Cameroonians who demanded autonomy and independence:

> Do they really imagine for example, that France, which is still suffering great financial difficulties because of the effort undertaken to pacify Algeria, is going to provide the billions needed for the construction of the "Douala-Chad" if it is only to put this magnificent tool of development into inexpert hands in six years, at the very moment when France should leave Cameroon when the latter will have achieved total independence, no doubt refusing even a federalist form?
>
> One does not start expensive works on a building which is going to be expropriated. Under these conditions it is more than likely that the "Douala-Chad" will never be constructed. There is enough to do, if one wants to spend money in the other territories of French Africa which are basically faithful to the *métropole* and where the word autonomy has never been pronounced.[4]

The other possibility was to leave the rail network as it was since it served the limited zone of Cameroon, which in any case was the only area of real economic interest to the French. For thirty years the French postponed the plan to construct a railway from Douala to Chad, but as the necessary political conditions never quite materialized, the railway continued to serve only Cameroon. French colonial interests were concentrated in one tenth of the territory served by the railway, that is to say in the production area of the main cash crops of Cameroon. This zone, in the shape of a semi-circle with a radius of 300-350 km from Douala, became so essential for French economic plans in Cameroon, that it was referred to as the "fertile crescent."

> The fertile crescent extends its two horns from Foumban to Abong Mbang and its curve follows in general the railway line from Nkongsamba to Bonabéri and from Douala to Mbalmayo. The towns of Dschang, Nkongsamba, Loum, Edéa, Ebolowa, Sangmélima are part of the fertile crescent which extends from the Bamiléképland to the southern zone.
> The southern zone is a "fertile crescent" whose two endpoints reach the Yaoundé region to the East, and the mountainous zone of Bamilékéland to the west and ends in Foumban. The center of the crescent is Douala and the two branches are separated by the Wouri River.
> The fertile crescent has approximately 1,500,000 inhabitants. All the rich products are found here: cocoa, coffee, banana as well as natural resources: palm trees and forests.[5]

Despite frequent references to the *mise en valeur* (development) of Cameroon, the French were so concerned with the "fertile crescent" that one author went as far as to call it *le Cameroun utile* (useful Cameroon).[6] Even André Soucadaux, the High-Commissioner, described the area as a *cercle utile* (useful circle).[7] As a result, the greater part of their infrastructural investments was devoted not to the development of Cameroon into a viable economic unit, but to the construction of facilities for the export of cash crops and the import of industrial products, in keeping with what could be referred to as the "policy of the fertile crescent."

In this respect, the data in table 9.1 and figure 9.1 showing the regional breakdown of the FIDES loans from 1946 to 1956 are instructive. In view of the role of the port of Douala in the development and exploitation of the "fertile crescent" and the French territories surrounding Cameroon, the importance accorded to the Wouri region, with Douala as its capital, appears very clearly in these figures, but is no longer surprising. With only 3.8 percent of the Cameroonian population and 0.3 percent of the territory, the Wouri region, whose production of either subsistence or export goods was insignificant in the economy of the territory, was favored significantly over other regions. The Wouri region benefited from 6,926 million CFA Francs, which represents nearly one third of the total loans FIDES granted to Cameroon from 1946 to 1956. It should also be noted that about eight tenths of the loans accorded to the Wouri region were invested in infrastructural development. Because of their importance for export production the Mungo and the Sanaga Maritime regions, with approximately 15 percent of loans each, came in second place, but far behind the Wouri region. As with the latter, more than 90

Figure 9.1

Distribution by region of FIDES loans in Cameroon from 1946 to 1956

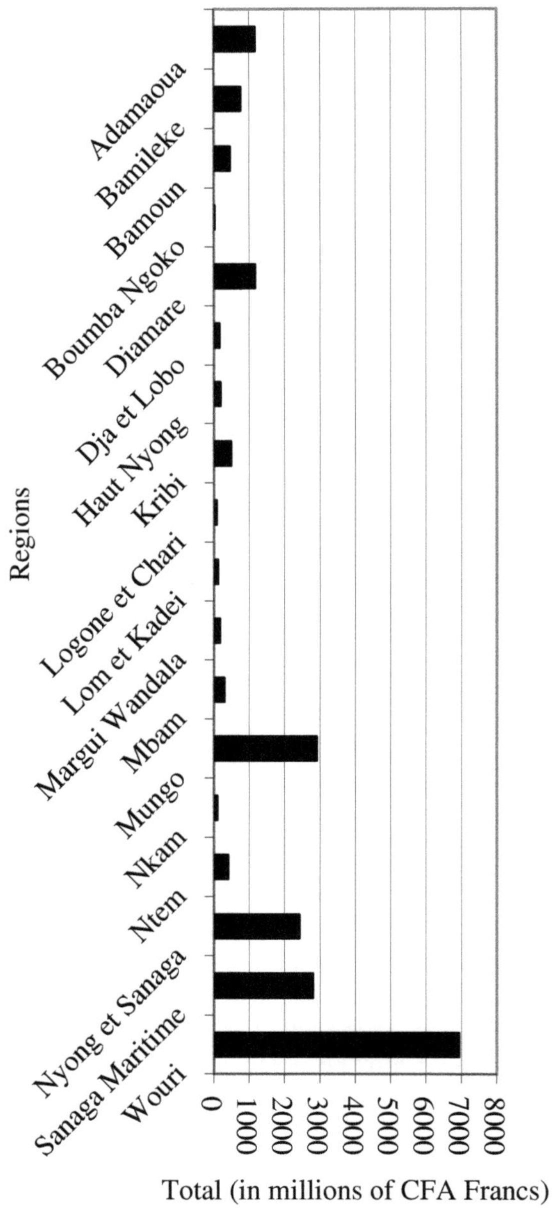

percent of the loans granted to the Sanaga Maritime region, and more than 80 percent of those going to the Mungo region, were invested in infrastructure.

Table 9.1

Regional distribution of FIDES loans in Cameroon from 1946 to 1956

	Adama-oua	Bamiléké	Bamoun	Boumba Ngoko	Diamaré
Population	178,175	464,616	90,960	25,000	413,700
Agricultural production	248.8	252.8	183.2	14.1	446.7
Transportation & communication	793.9	133.4	120.3	0.9	446.8
Social infrastructure	39.9	261	148.2	4.9	252.2
TOTAL	1,167.6	747.0	451.7	19.9	1,165.7

	Dja-et-Lobo	Haut-Nyong	Kribi	Logone-et-Chari	Margui-Wandala
Population	77,500	75,713	51,245	70,416	272,084
Agricultural production	108.4	57.1	72.8	50.6	144.1
Transportation & communication	4.1	100.4	389	14.0	5.6
Social infrastructure	35.1	18	13.7	10.8	14.4
TOTAL	147.6	175.5	475.7	73.3	164.1

	Mbam	Mungo	Nkam	Ntem
Population	108,000	110,977	37,007	94,846
Agricultural production	82.6	328.8	36.6	209.9
Transportation & communication	8.3	2,373.5	44.7	80.0
Social infrastructure	195.6	196.3	9.6	103.9
TOTAL	286.5	2,898.6	90.6	393.8

Table 9.1 *(Continued)*

	Nyong-et Sanaga	Sanaga Maritime	Wouri
Population	437,874	148,629	120,000
Agricultural production	602.3	101	112
Transportation and communication	693.2	2,539.3	5,586.5
Social infrastructure	1,118.6	153.9	1,197.5
TOTAL	2,413.9	2,794.2	6,926.0

Source: adapted from *ATCAM, Journal des débats*, Séance du 27 avril 1957, p. 498.
Population: Number of inhabitants
Agricultural production, transportation and communication, social infrastructure, and total: amounts in millions of CFA Francs.

Altogether three quarters of the loans allocated to infrastructure were invested in three regions, namely Wouri, Mungo and Sanaga Maritime, which contained only 13 percent of the population of Cameroon and less than 6 percent of the territory, while the fifteen other regions, occupying more than 94 percent of the territory and containing more than 86 percent of the population of Cameroon, shared the remaining one fourth.

Whenever the French sought to demonstrate the usefulness of the improvements brought to the infrastructure of Cameroon, they pointed first to the rise in exports and imports during this period. The figures of foreign trade of western Cameroon show that from 1946 to 1953 which was the period of large-scale infrastructural works, the quantity of Cameroonian exports increased from 132,430 tons in 1947 to 223,929 tons in 1950 and to 273,260 in 1953; during the same period imports rose from 77,030 tons in 1946 to 226,647 tons in 1950, to reach 287,788 tons in 1953. Figure 9.2 shows this development of Cameroon's imports and exports. However, the above figures which the French cited as proof of their positive contribution to the territory were increasingly seen by Cameroonians as a reinforcement of their subordinate position in the economic structure of French colonialism.[8]

The Plan pursued the policy of the "fertile crescent" not only in the infrastructural area but also in all other areas, including that of social development. While water systems were installed at Nkongsamba, Edéa, Douala, and Yaoundé, the other towns of the interior were given the bare minimum. Whereas the hospitals of Douala and Yaoundé were provided with significant additional equipment (in hospital wards, maternity wings, pharmacies,

Figure 9.2

Development of Cameroon imports and exports from 1947 to 1953

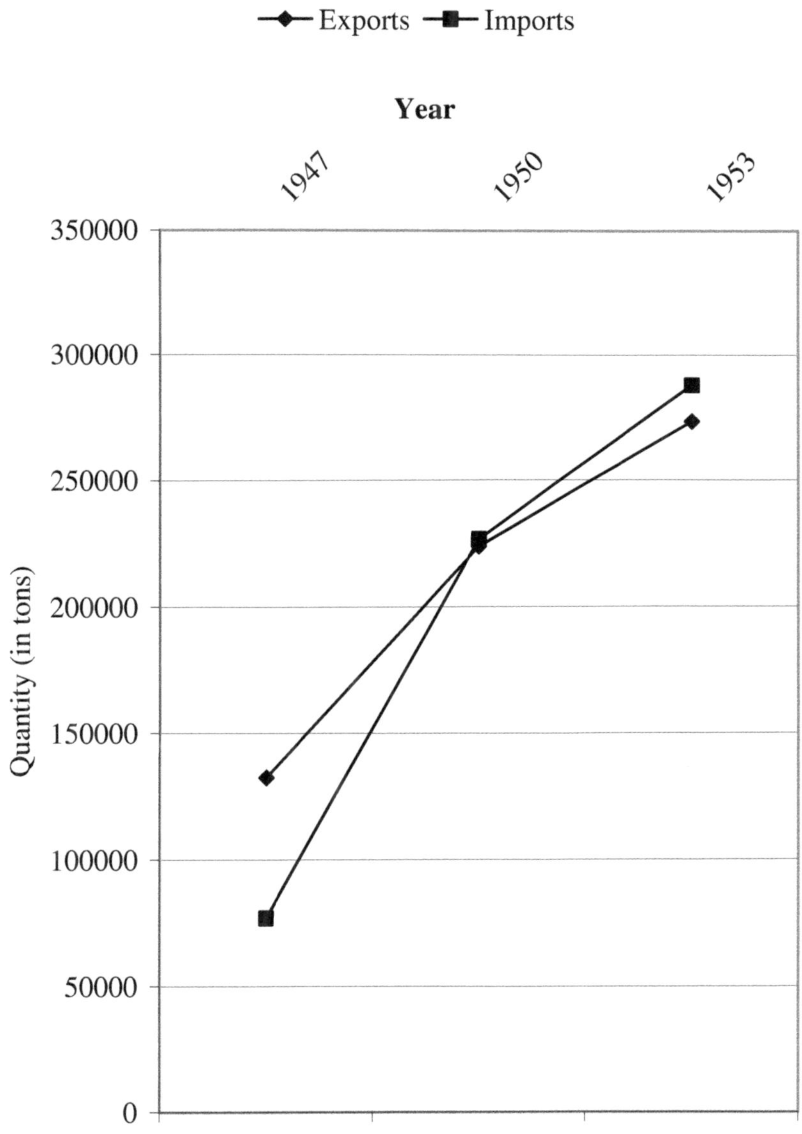

etc.), the other regions were granted only 19 hospital wards, 17 dispensaries, and 6 maternity hospitals. The same orientation appeared in the field of education: one high school (*lycée*) in Yaoundé, two secondary establishments in Douala and Nkongsamba, two primary schools in Douala and Yaoundé, and for the rest of the country only regional and rural primary schools and a middle school in Garoua.[9]

Such a policy was not in keeping with the law of April 30, 1946. This law called for the harmonious development of all economic and social activities, the final goal being "to primarily satisfy the needs of the native population and to create the most favorable conditions for their social progress." But it became clear that these guidelines were not applied in Cameroon, for the French did not seek the harmonious development of the Cameroonian economy. Instead they embarked on a large-scale program of construction which was completed within seven or eight years. This meant the rapid transformation of the employment structure of the Cameroonian population who lived in the vicinity of these major projects, as thousands gave up their marginal farming or other activities to seek work in the construction and ancillary concerns that proliferated. Moreover, the construction program acted as a magnet for French capital and for foreign companies as well as for the Europeans of the country, who rushed to profit from the manna by setting up tool shops, repair shops, or simply garages. Since there was no other program likely to provide a continuation there was considerable anxiety among both Cameroonians and European settlers when this construction program ended.

Finally, if one looks more closely, it appears that the FIDES was not as generous as it first appeared. The program involved a 45 percent contribution by the territory based largely on loans from CCFOM, a percentage that was to decrease over time. The estimates of the contributions of Cameroon to the development plans for the 1946–1958 period vary from one author to another. According to Willard Johnson, these contributions amounted to 64,579 million French Francs, that is to say, a little more than 40 percent of the total investment for the period from 1946 to 1958.[10] Abel Eyinga gives a much higher estimate of 71,906 billion French Francs for Cameroon's contribution to FIDES from 1947 to 1957.[11]

Whatever source is used, it seems that not only was this program designed by France to meet French colonial needs, but also as a means of investing Cameroonian financial resources in French companies. Thus, Cameroon was shareholder in the companies created in its territory according to the law of April 30, 1946. It contributed to financing these companies in exchange for a representation on their board of directors. Table 9.2 sh[ows] Cameroon's contribution to the capital of these companies until Decem[ber]

Table 9.2

Cameroon's contribution to the capital of French public companies. Situation by December 31, 1956.

	Capital	Cameroon's contribution	Percentage
CREDICAM	350	135	38.8%
ENELCAM	1,900	189	9.8%
SIC	100	35	35.0%
SEREPCA	3,200	360	11.2%

Source: ANSOM, FIDES 351, "Le plan et l'évolution du Cameroun, 1947–1956," p. 102.

31, 1956. As the trade union leader Jacques Ngom put it, "FIDES was a suction pump, not a pump to supply the African basin."[12] And many Cameroonians agreed with Um Nyobè that: "FIDES only benefits private companies under government control."[13]

The FIDES which the French often wanted to present as a disinterested initiative of a state which was above private interests, was actually a mechanism designed to favor the exportation of French capital. During the 1950s this exportation of capital accompanied by direct investment was of great importance at a moment when there was competition among rival capitalist groups for the control of markets and raw materials. The technique of project realization was based on a simple principle: public capital was exported in close association with private capital. The former served generally as basic investment the management of which was not profitable. The latter went to companies which made use of significant installations at low cost thanks to public loans and as a result made high profit. The best example of this practice in Cameroon is that of the *Compagnie Camerounaise de l'Aluminium Pechiney-Ugine* known as ALUCAM.

ALUCAM: To Serve the French Economy

During the period under study, ALUCAM was one of the largest French projects in Cameroon. This project was born in the wake of the crisis the French aluminum industry faced in the 1950s. French authorities clearly defined the purpose of establishing an aluminum factory in Cameroon: to safeguard the advance of the French aluminum industry whose rise has been ·cked by both qualitative and quantitative exhaustion of metropolitan rces of bauxite, and even more importantly by the rising cost of electricity in the *métropole*.[14] Therefore, if the French turned towards Black Africa, it was primarily to look for cheap electricity which their aluminum industry urgently needed in order to avoid a metal shortage in their market and to be able to continue exporting. Africa offered enormous under-exploited hydroelectric reserves. France explored the possibility of creating dams on the Konkouré River in Guinea and on the Kouilou River in Middle Congo. But prompted by the rising need for aluminum, the choice fell on Edéa which offered an immediate solution.[15]

The hydroelectric and metallurgical complex at Edéa, approximately 80 km from Douala, required first the building of a dam on the Sanaga River and generators to provide electricity by ENELCAM, and then the construction of a plant for the processing of alumina into aluminum by the *Compagnie Camerounaise de l'Aluminium Péchiney-Ugine* (ALUCAM). As a result, the capacity of the hydroelectric plant of Edéa which until 1953 was 20,000 kw grew to 125,000 kw of which 105,000 kw were going to be used by ALUCAM.[16]

While the average price of the kilowatt per hour in the French Union was 15 French Francs as opposed to 3 to 4 francs in France, and the domestic consumer of Edéa had to pay 56 to 60 francs, Edéa provided electricity to the subsidiary of Péchiney at 0.8 francs, with a decrease to 0.74 beginning in 1966.[17] Clearly, as an observer mentioned, "ALUCAM was established in Cameroon because the Edéa dam could supply electricity at a cost unavailable in Europe."[18] Also, ALUCAM enjoyed other advantages: the new company was guaranteed stable tax conditions for fifteen years and customs duty would apply neither to aluminum imported from France or Guinea nor to exported aluminum.

The project was to cost an estimated 26 billion CFA Francs, of which about 70 percent came from public funds, including Cameroon's contributions. The participation of the territory in the investments and then the expected profits from ALUCAM was only 8 percent, as opposed to 10 percent for CCFOM and 82 percent for the French firm Péchiney-Ugine.[19] The project became operational in 1956 and was expected to eventually produce 45,000 tons of aluminum per year.

The French often presented ALUCAM not only as an impressive technological achievement, but also as a symbol of the disappearance of the former colonial relationship. ALUCAM functioned as follows: in the region of Marseilles, bauxite was transformed into an intermediate product, alumina; this alumina was then shipped to Cameroon where it was processed by the ALUCAM plant and the aluminum, thus produced, was sent back to France, where it was used to manufacture industrial or household goods. At the opening ceremony of the dam of Edéa on February 5, 1954, Louis Jacquinot, then Minister of Overseas France, declared:

> Among the industrial projects, the most important one will lead to an immediate need to increase the capacity of the plant at Edéa, in order to be able to process tens of thousands of tons of aluminum coming from the *métropole*. For the first time the traditional pattern of exporting raw materials from the territories to the *métropole* and manufactured products from the *métropole* towards the overseas territories will be reversed. This time the *métropole* will be processing its own raw materials overseas. I hope that this example will be mulled over by all those who accuse us of still practicing the colonial pact.[20]

Jacquinot offered these comforting words about the project because many Cameroonians began to take a closer look at it and were alarmed by what they discovered. Although the construction of the electrical and industrial complex of Edéa made possible the hiring of 2 to 3,000 Cameroonian workers, the project was going to employ only 600 Cameroonians and 100 French technical and managerial personnel when completed.[21] Yet, Edéa is located in the heart of the Bassaà country in the Sanaga Maritime region, and the Bassaà were one of the Cameroonian peoples most affected by unemployment. Thus, ALUCAM was an example of a French capital-intensive project which, nonetheless, created only a limited amount of employment. Many Cameroonians were not impressed. In a study on the social impact of ALUCAM, William Etéki Mboumoua gives the results of a survey he carried out among a number of Cameroonians on the image of this company:

> More than 70 percent were even unaware of the existence of an aluminum plant at Edéa. About 30 percent had some idea....Approximately three fifths of this 30 percent thought that ALUCAM exploited the resources of the country...in short an example of capitalist imperialism. Because, they said, electricity was delivered to ALUCAM at the price of 0.35 CFA Francs while the price for the consumers was set by ENELCAM at 29 CFA Francs, which one may call exorbitant in a country where the standard of living is low. Obviously those who held this view were mostly unaware that...the 0.35 francs was the price above which Péchiney-Ugine would not take any risk for the company since it would not have been profitable.
>
> In the eyes of the majority of the population, ALUCAM retains the regrettable characteristics of a colonial capitalist company, without anything new to add to the common good.[22]

Many observers thought that ALUCAM benefited Cameroon only marginally or not at all. But was it built for Cameroon? Péchiney-Ugine was also involved in constructing a plant in Guinea which, it was hoped, would later provide alumina to Cameroon. Cameroonians could thus consider ALUCAM to be a symbol of French neo-colonialism. This consideration is based on the view of such French experts as René Dumont who stated that the capitalists deliberately chose to produce alumina in Guinea and aluminum in

Cameroon in order to avoid the risk of nationalization.[23] Moreover, a careful examination of ALUCAM and ENELCAM highlights the way the French sought to structure Cameroon's economy to serve the needs of France. The French usually considered the complex of Edéa to be "a step forward" in colonial economic relations, not in the sense suggested by Louis Jacquinot, but because ALUCAM functioned very much like other French aluminum producing plants. Far from being a reversal of colonialism, ALUCAM demonstrated how it could be pushed to its logical extreme.

> The alumina will come from France, that is to say that the plant in Cameroon will be supplied with this raw material as any French aluminum producing factory installed in the Alps or the Pyrenees.[24]

In the eyes of Péchiney-Ugine and the French Government, ALUCAM added a new colonial resource to the cheap workforce, raw materials and a large market: the supplying of cheap electricity for French industrial concerns. At the time of the construction of the Edéa complex the French predicted that the production of electricity would far outstrip the needs of ALUCAM and could thus serve as the basis for an industrialization plan which would go beyond providing cheap electricity to a few processing industries. When the French ministers addressed a public other than the Cameroonian one, it appeared clearly that the French Government was above all concerned with resolving the problems of French industry with the help of Cameroonian capital and natural resources. The following report published in *Climats* is a good example:

> M. Buron explains that in France the price of the industrial kilowatt is too high for the heavy and metallic industries using electricity as a raw material....The lowest price available in metropolitan France, the minister indicated, is 3 francs. Whereas, if we consider the experience of Edéa, one can estimate that 16 billion kilowatts could be supplied by Black Africa and Madagascar at the price of 0.80 francs [per kilowatt].[25]

The attitude of those who blamed the Plan for primarily serving the large companies and maintaining a system of profit-making and domination can also be understood. In the Cameroonian case this state of mind was altogether understandable because of the relatively weak impact of ALUCAM on local revenues and the territorial budget. Péchiney's subsidiary could neither contribute to nor balance the Cameroonian budget, nor could it solve the problem of full employment. In a report which he published in the *Figaro* in 1957, Lecerf explained why ALUCAM could not bring a decisive contribution to Cameroon:

> It [ALUCAM] will increase the traffic of the port of Douala and one tenth of that of the railways. It will provide taxes but a long-term agreement aimed at facilitating the establishment of the company will limit the amount. It will give a salary to about 400 Africans, which is not too many, and one can ask what will be done with the 1,200 workers currently employed in the building of the site.... The interest of the project lies elsewhere. It is first of all to provide us with aluminum which is much needed in the franc zone.[26]

After Cameroon attained independence on January 1, 1960 the situation did not change at all, as noted by Philippe Hugon, a French economist:

> ALUCAM has no effect on the hinterland (it exclusively uses the aluminum of Fria, and its whole production is re-exported). The manufacturing of aluminum articles by Socatral and Alubassa is done with imported aluminum. ALUCAM distributes in the form of salaries 5 percent of its earnings. Exempt from taxes, ALUCAM repatriates the quasi totality of its profits. It utilizes almost exclusively a dam financed by public funds and pays a rate of 0.50 francs per kilowatt hour for an operating cost of 11 francs.[27]

The following remark perfectly summarized the experience of the Cameroonian subsidiary of Péchiney-Ugine: "ALUCAM is not a Cameroonian problem solved by Péchiney. It is a problem of Péchiney solved in Cameroon."[28]

Inequalities in the Semi-Industrial, Commercial and Agricultural Sectors

One of the direct consequences of the investment program of the French Government beginning in 1947 was to stimulate investments by private European concerns in the territory. There were two main reasons for this: first, many of the FIDES funds went directly to European-owned production enterprises, and favored the establishment of ancillary concerns which serviced the construction effort; second, by the early 1950s, Cameroon had acquired a strong reputation among the French for its investment potential. With the failure of colonial plans elsewhere, especially in Indochina, Cameroon became a favored target for investors, a refuge for available capital. The favored status of Cameroon in French Black Africa with regard to private investments within the framework of the FIDES program has already been demonstrated in the preceding chapter.

But whereas the large public investments in Cameroon engendered a criticism of French colonialism in the territory mostly by radicals, the considerable private investments led to similar misgivings among the more bourgeois and moderate nationalists.[29] This is explained by the fact that the industrial projects which were to be established in the "fertile crescent" were entirely controlled by Europeans. This was due to the logic of the capitalist system. To establish the smallest forestry or mining concern, even one of an artisanal nature, loans were necessary. But the required conditions to be granted a loan were made in a way that one had to first possess significant wealth. This meant that in the final analysis loaning institutions lent to the wealthy only, that is to say, to Europeans, who were the only ones able to provide the required guarantees. The indigenous poor could not manage to obtain even the smallest amounts. In a letter addressed to the United Nations Secretary General on November 25, 1954, Daniel Kémajou denounced this situation when he wrote:

> The Cameroonian is very poor because banks and loaning institutions do not extend their facilities to the autochthonous Cameroonians to allow them to make their businesses work.[30]

Charles Okala, who appeared before the Fourth Committee of the United Nations along with Um Nyobè in 1952, expressed the increasing anxiety of those Cameroonians who felt frustrated by the European domination of the economy of the territory. Here is a summary of his intervention:

> Okala deplores the fact that the Europeans monopolized the economy, that the administering authority does not encourage the cooperative movement and affordable credit and that, in practice, *Crédit du Cameroun* grants loans only to Europeans and only for construction projects. He thinks that the profits made by the middlemen are excessive and he wishes the considerable profit foreign companies derive from the sale of cocoa and other products were rather invested within the country. He notes with regret the failure of the *Sociétés Indigènes de Prévoyance*.[31]

To have an even clearer idea of the preoccupations of Cameroonians the 26-page long memorandum addressed to the UN by the Ngondo, the traditional Assembly of the Duala people, on November 26, 1949 can be cited:

> Does the transfer of super-profits made in the territory to French banks constitute the proper application of the United Nations Charter which thus allows them to abandon their duty which should have been local reinvestment in order to make possible the economic growth and development of local opportunities for production? These profits could be made thanks to the richness of the land and the joint work of Europeans and indigenous people. It would be fair if they were returned to the local economy for the greatest possible benefit of all. Any transfer policies deprive the territory of the financial means indispensable for its own development.

Besides the fact that the European companies of Cameroon transferred their profits to France instead of reinvesting them locally, the abusive granting by the French Administration of land concessions to private European concerns to the detriment of the autochthonous population was another significant grievance which appeared in the memorandum of the Ngondo:

> We have enormous wealth in our territory. All the wealth is ceded in a definitive and exclusive fashion to the large European companies and firms.
> In Cameroon some agricultural and forestry companies, some twenty large planters share four fifths of the forests and the arable land among themselves.
> A choice has to be made between a policy which grants large concessions to Europeans and one which stimulates local initiatives. Cameroon opts for the latter.

The problem of the industrialization of their country was not absent from the economic concerns of Cameroonians:

> It is no longer possible to continue to forbid or to hold back the industrialization of the territory under the fallacious pretext that this industrialization would create competition for the corresponding industries of France. We have all kinds of natural products here, which if manufactured locally could greatly help to raise the indigenous people's living standards.

The memorandum of the Ngondo expressed a feeling which was common among many Cameroonians, that is, a desire for collaboration between the indigenous population and the Europeans. However, the memorandum did not explain the different conceptions Cameroonians had of this collaboration.

> It is no longer possible to continue the conflict between the Europeans who have the financial and technical means and the indigenous people, the owners of the land and the sub-soil who offer their arms, their knowledge of the country and their own adaptation to the climate and to the living conditions of the territory.[32]

What was most exasperating for Cameroonians and some Europeans was, on the one hand, the superficial nature of the investments,[33] and, on the other, the wastefulness represented by unnecessary construction work, undertaken simply because the money came from the public treasury. The criticism did not come from the local assembly which usually ratified everything the authorities submitted to it, but from other elements in the country who strongly complained about the waste of public funds in the unnecessary projects undertaken by private companies. These were primarily the *colons* (settlers) established for some years in the territory, owners of middle level and often marginal concerns, who did not benefit from the enormous profits reaped by large construction companies which came to the territory to implement the Plan. As an example of misallocation of funds the *colons* and some Cameroonians often mentioned the *Route Razel* (Razel Road) constructed between Douala and Edéa. In their view this project was absolutely unnecessary since there was already a road which could have been improved for a fraction of the two billion CFA Francs spent on the building of a road which was only ten kilometers longer than the one it replaced.[34]

Thus the *colons* were pitted against the *hommes du Plan* (the Plan men) whom they considered to be the allies of large international companies involved in major construction work. This conflict perpetuated the post-war tension which appeared clearly in the *Etats Généraux de la Colonisation Française* and the Association of the *Colons* of Cameroon (ASCOCAM), and foreshadowed more violent clashes later when the small investors became the first to suffer from the decline of large-scale investment.

In the commercial sector the situation was similar to that existing elsewhere in French Black Africa. The greater part of wholesale and retail trade was controlled by major colonial trading firms which were found elsewhere in West Africa, whereas the middle level of both the retail trade and the purchasing of agricultural produce was in the hands of Greeks and Lebanese. The competition was too strong for Cameroonians who complained that this situation was putting them in a disadvantageous position.

> The open door policy is applied rather cavalierly. The Government grants the facilities to all Europeans and the large commercial companies favor small European retail traders.
> This competition organized blindly and unfairly will bring the autochthonous traders to the abyss.
> The economic policy of the Administration is suffused with the same tendencies as pure politics. Many French had already made their fortune in our country and had gone to live off their wealth in the *métropole*.
> The material difficulties faced by Cameroonian enterprises are compounded by financial and especially fiscal ones, the solution to which clearly does not depend on the traders and exploiters. On the one hand transportation weighs heavily on Cameroonian products and imported goods are taxed with excessive charges; on the other hand an overly harsh tax system compromises any possibility for the eventual development of commercial or other undertakings.
> As for banks, they systematically refuse to grant any loans to the indigenous people.[35]

The unwillingness of banks to grant loans to Cameroonians to allow them to enter local or import-export trade, and the procrastination of the Administration in the granting of necessary licenses pushed many moderate Cameroonians who had remained on the sidelines of the anti-colonial struggle until 1953 towards a more nationalist position.

The only group that experienced progress among the Cameroonian population was the Bamiléké group who made considerable advances in the commercial domain despite innumerable difficulties. This was in part due to their economic dynamism, and in part to their highly developed methods for pooling their financial resources, allowing them to sidestep the discriminatory policies of banks and other credit institutions in Cameroon. But when the Bamiléké reached the middle levels of the commercial sector, they were faced with competition from Greeks, other Europeans, or Lebanese, and this was one of the factors contributing to their support for the anti-colonial movement.

During the decade following the Second World War the agricultural sector saw a rapid growth in the production and export of commercial crops. It is interesting to examine the three main export crops, cocoa, coffee and bananas which represented 70 percent of the exports value. Their production zones were distinct. Coffee and banana plantations were concentrated along the Western frontier with bananas exclusively found in the Mungo region, while coffee was found throughout the region up to Foumbot in the Bamoun region. Cocoa was most successful in the central and southern regions of the territory from Yaoundé to Ebolowa and Ambam in the south. To this geographical division another almost racial division was added, since until the Second World War European farmers retained a monopoly on bananas and coffee which was only broken during the post-war period by Cameroonians, mostly Bamiléké, who eventually succeeded in sharing the export market equally with Europeans. By contrast, cocoa production had since 1930 been 100 percent controlled by Cameroonians.

Calculations made from the official figures of the value of Cameroonian exports from 1946 to 1956 (see table 8.2) show that during the period under study cocoa alone represented 50 percent of the total exports, while coffee and bananas amounted to 20 percent. The considerable growth in the value of the export earnings of these three crops guaranteed the prosperity of the concerned areas by comparison with neighboring regions. The remaining 30 percent of exports was divided basically as follows: 5.6 percent for timber, 3.6 percent for cotton; 2.8 percent for rubber; 2.8 percent for palm oil and palm kernels; 1.8 percent for peanuts; and 1 percent for tobacco. The main minerals tin, titanium and gold amounted to less than 0.3 percent of the value of exports. These numbers clearly indicate the importance of the three main cash crops. It must be noted that from 1938 to 1955 cocoa production doubled, coffee production increased two and a half times, and that of bananas trebled. Figure 9.3 shows the development of the value of the main Cameroonian exports.

The French Administration vigorously encouraged Cameroonians to cultivate cocoa in the regions where the soil and the climate allowed it. "Quite clearly, the enthusiasm of the administration for cocoa cultivation derived from the assumption that it would lead to the *embourgeoisement* of a significant Cameroonian middle class: Cameroonians on whom the French could anchor their rule."[36] Cocoa plants can be found throughout the "fertile crescent," but the crop is concentrated to a remarkable extent in the zone inhabited

Figure 9.3

Development of the value of the main Cameroon exports from 1946 to 1956

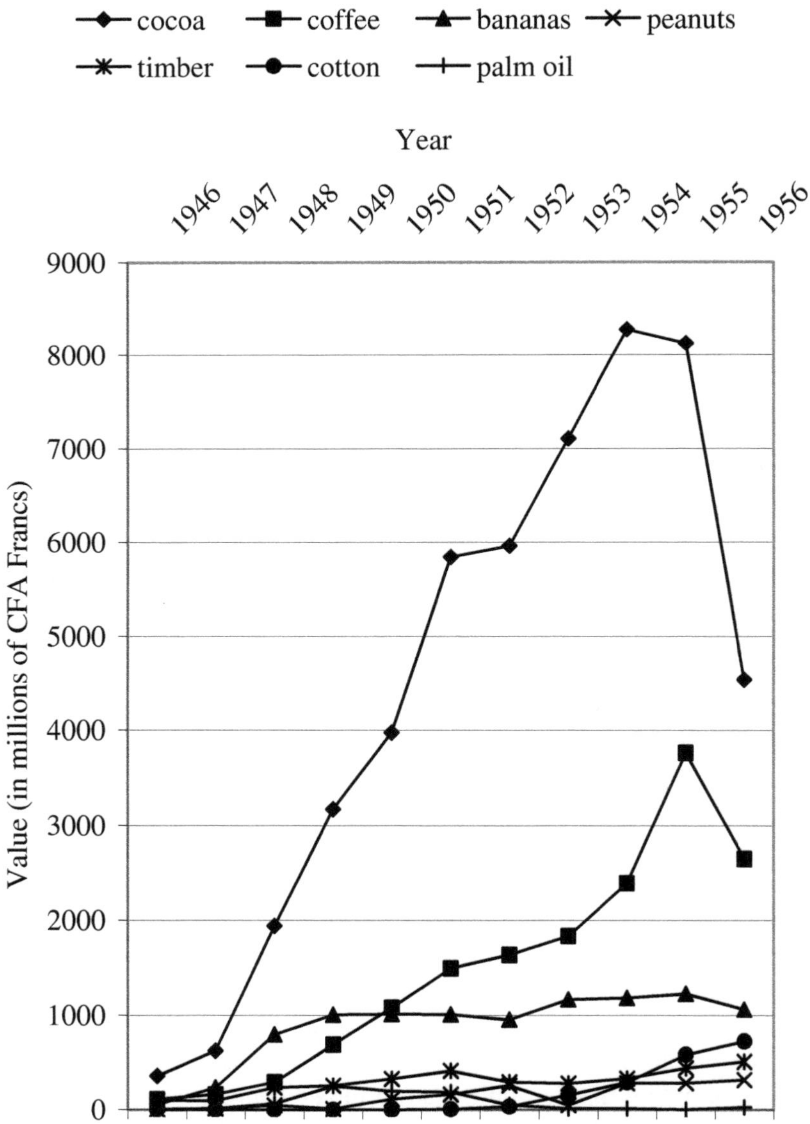

by the Beti-Pahouin peoples (the administrative districts of Nyong-et-Sanaga, Ntem, and Dja-et-Lobo). In 1950, 92,000 of the 120,000 hectares producing cocoa were to be found in this zone.

The other important characteristic of cocoa in Cameroon, apart from its localization, was its crucial role in the economy of the territory. There were two main reasons for this. First, given the relatively high population density of the cocoa growing zone and the small size of individual holdings, it can be estimated that about 150,000 peasants lived from this crop. If we add to this number the families, clerks and truck drivers whose livelihood derived from buying and transporting this crop, we can see that more than 500,000 Cameroonians depended on cocoa. Second, as cocoa represented 50 percent of exports, the entire economy was based on the world price of this crop, which however was not guaranteed at all. The crucial significance of cocoa exports meant the prosperity of a large portion of the rural areas until 1955, and the discontent of the same group as a result of the fall in the price of cocoa in 1955–1956.

If Cameroonians controlled the cocoa sector, the situation was very different for the other two crops. After the Great Depression of 1929, European settlers turned towards bananas and coffee, having discovered that the western highlands of the Bamiléké and Bamoun regions offered ideal circumstances for the cultivation of coffee, especially for the growing of the profitable Arabica variety, while the volcanic soils of the Mungo region proved excellent for banana cultivation. To a lesser degree, some Europeans continued to cultivate tobacco and to exploit palm products.

Cameroonian production of coffee reached 60 percent of the total, whereas in the case of bananas, European production was generally more important than that of the Africans.[37] The unequal nature of the competition in this zone does not appear clearly from the statistical sources because during much of the period under study here, there was a discriminatory quota system in force which allowed Europeans to export a larger portion of their production than Cameroonians. In addition, the method of selecting bananas for export worked against Cameroonian producers who were, therefore, very dissatisfied with the system.

Between 1951 and 1955, Europeans doubled the amount of coffee they produced, while banana production decreased slowly. Moreover, the areas cultivated by Africans increased substantially for both crops. It must be understood that the system of cultivation of the Cameroonians differed greatly from that of the Europeans. The latter practiced a more intensive form of agriculture which used more artificial fertilizers and insecticides than their Cameroonian competitors who planted banana and coffee interspersed with food crops. Thus the Europeans obtained much higher yields.

There were close links between international trading companies and the local associations of European farmers for the sale and shipping of bananas. In the case of the sale of coffee these transactions were less delicate in nature and thus the organizational advantage of Europeans was not as important in this sector. Thanks to the activities of their SIPs and other co-operatives Cameroonians were able to outstrip Europeans in the sale of coffee in the early 1950s. In the case of bananas Europeans resisted more firmly. Not only were Europeans able to utilize their existing organizational system to exclude many of their African competitors but they could also use the quota system as a politico-administrative weapon. When in 1946, the banana production of the Cameroonians reached a level that permitted them to be included in the export trade, a government decree assigned them a quota of 15 percent. This quota was raised to 21 percent in 1949 and then to 27.5 percent in 1950.[38] In each case, this increase was only a compromise, which did not reflect the rise in production of the Cameroonians. The competition was all the more lively as the area cultivated by the Cameroonians doubled while that of the Europeans began to decline.

In this part of the territory where cash crop production was very well developed, the exasperation of Cameroonians caused by the competition among European planters, Bamiléké pioneers and local peoples had political consequences. As wealthy Bamiléké were looking to obtain political power to match their economic situation, the increasingly frequent use of Bamiléké emblems and the electoral mobilization of Bamiléké commoners could be observed. The other peoples also began to organize themselves politically. It was thus that the Mungo region became the site of some of the bloodiest atrocities during the Bamiléké stage of the Cameroonian rebellion which started in 1958. The armed struggle which broke out early in May 1955 was the first sign of the insurrection that by the end of the month was to initiate a period of revolutionary violence in the territory.

NOTES

1. Blanchet (A.), "L'avenir du territoire sera-t-il dans l'agriculture, les mines ou l'industrie ?" *Le Monde* (October 14, 1949): 8.
2. *Climats*, 442 (June 1954): 3.
3. "Rapport Annuel du Gouvernement Français" (1952), p. 75, and (1955), p. 72.
4. "Le Cameroun sans la France est un enfant mort-né," *Le Cameroun Libre*, 520 (July 1–15, 1955): 2.
5. *Climats*, 2 (July 1953): 17 and 21.

6. Hugon (P.), p. 14.
7. *ARCAM*, "séance extraordinaire du 17 au 21 janvier 1951. Procès verbaux des séances," p. 21.
8. See Eyinga (A.), "Dix années de FIDES," p. 19.
9. *Ibid*, p.20
10. Johnson (W.R.), *The Cameroon Federation: political integration in a fragmentary society* (Princeton, N.J: Princeton University Press, 1970), p. 108.
11. Eyinga (A.), "Dix années de FIDES," p. 16.
12. "Exploitation et lutte du peuple camerounais," *Cahiers Internationaux*, 54 (January 1954): 84.
13. ANCAM, 1 AC 19(5). The Secretary General of UPC made this statement during a press conference on May 12, 1954.
14. ANSOM, FIDES 77 (March 13, 1954 presentation on the establishment of an aluminium factory in Cameroon). See also Hoffher (R.), "Le Cameroun, exportateur d'énergie," *Marchés Coloniaux* (June 5, 1954): 1570; Hoffher was then the Director of Economic Affairs at the Ministry of Overseas France.
15. On the Sanaga River at Edéa there were waterfalls which were very large and easy to canalize. Moreover, that area already had a hydroelectric plant which offered an opportunity for easy extension.
16. *Chronique d'Outre Mer*, 7 (July 1954): 62.
17. "Les trusts français aux colonies," *Economie et politique*, 5–6 (1954): 102; Suret-Canale (J.), p. 270.
18. "Cameroun 1959," *Marchés Tropicaux et Méditerranéens*, 732 (November 21, 1959): 2585.
19. *Climats*, 448 (July 15–21, 1954): 17.
20. *Marchés Coloniaux*, 431 (February 13, 1954): 459; *Climats*, 426 (February 11–17, 1954): 3.
21. Etéki Mboumoua (W.), "De quelques incidents sociaux de l'ALUCAM," ENFOM, 64 (1958-59): 14.
22. *Ibid.*, p. 42–44.
23. Joseph (R.), p. 129.
24. "La création d'une industrie d'aluminium," *Chroniques d'Outre Mer*, 11 (January 1955): 62.
25. "La politique de M. Robert Buron outre mer," *Climats*, 460 (October 14–20, 1954): 3. R. Buron at the time was Minister of Overseas France.
26. Lecerf (M.), "Edéa, test de possibilité industrielle de l'Afrique," *Le Figaro* (March 15, 1957).
27. Hugon (P.), p. 121.
28. Moussa (P.), p. 159.
29. These private investments were basically made in the light industries: sawmills, palm oil refineries, bottling, and tobacco. On a lower level there were numerous car repair shops, plumbing and electric repair shops.
30. ANCAM, 1 AC 19(5).
31. "Ce que veut le peuple camerounais," Paris, 1952, p. 75.
32. ANU, RAG–2/130–75, file 130/5/03, "Assemblée Représentative du Cameroun," pp. 13-14.
33. "Les crédits du FIDES auront une fin," *Le Cameroun Libre*, 422 (May 1, 1952): 2.
34. See: *Climats*, 342 (July 2-8, 1952); *Le Cameroun Libre*, 496 (July 1-15, 1955); and C. Okala's statement at ATCAM in 1957 (*ATCAM, Journal des débats...* Séance du 27 avril 1957, p. 519).

35. ANU, RAG–2/130–75, file 130/5/03. Memorandum of the Ngondo, pp. 14-16.
36. Atangana (M), "Capitalism and Nationalism in Cameroon," *African Studies Review*, Vol. 40, 1 (April 1997): 85.
37. Joseph (R.), p. 137.
38. Maslin (Ph.), "Peuplement blanc et mise en valeur de l'ouest Cameroun," ENFOM, 20 (1951-52), p. 27.

Conclusion

This book has sought to understand the role played by Cameroon in the dynamics of French capitalism, and also the role played by French capitalism in the development of Cameroon. To reach that goal the movements of capital between Cameroon and France and especially the exportation of French capital to Cameroon, and the impact of French investment in Cameroon in the decade that followed the Second World War were assessed.

The analysis offered in this work showed that France exported to Cameroon a considerable amount of capital which allowed the launching of significant projects and the growth of private European investment. However, the unfolding of French capitalism in this part of the colonial Empire also created hardships and imbalances, which contributed to and amplified growing discontent in the mid-1950s. The UPC's demands for independence and the increasing support which the nationalist movement enjoyed from a large part of the Cameroonian population seemed to be an expression of this discontent. From 1946 to 1956 the image of France gradually deteriorated in Cameroon despite the important metropolitan financial effort made in a territory which had a strong anti-colonial tradition since German colonization. Cameroon remains one of the most striking examples of anti-colonialism in tropical Africa. In 1956 anti-colonialism in Cameroon deteriorated into a state of war.

The mismanaged policy of the governments of the Fourth Republic and French investments were responsible for the growth of nationalism and rebellion in Cameroon in many ways. The intensive infrastructural work undertaken by France, the growth of private capital investment, and the steady rise in the production of the main export crops contrasted with the inertia of the French in the political field. Between 1950 and 1955, little or no progress was made towards granting legislative power to the local assembly, establishing a democratic system of local government, or organizing free elections in the territory.

The disparity between the scale of economic activity and the degree of political advancement was also apparent in other spheres. After the Second World War, Cameroonians who benefited from the high level of educational achievement created by French investment found themselves confronted with the intensification of European domination in the principal employment sectors to which they aspired, namely the civil service and private enterprise. In the agricultural sector of banana and coffee cultivation whose share of the export market was artificially protected, the dynamic Bamiléké agricultural producers began to realize that their economic advancement was hindered by the colonial state and its nationals. Even in the cocoa growing region where agriculture was completely in Cameroonian hands, the disparity between this control and the European and Greco-Lebanese domination of economic transactions finally exasperated the Cameroonian population of this region, especially when the cocoa boom ended in 1955.

It was the Bassaà people who paid the highest price for the inherent contradictions of colonial domination. Along with Douala, the Bassaà region was simultaneously the scene of the most important investment projects including ALUCAM and ENELCAM, and one of the most economically depressed areas in the south, especially in terms of salaries. It is not difficult to understand, therefore, that the Bassaà became ready recruits for the UPC's guerilla army.

The emerging stratum of entrepreneurs, which was the driving force of most nationalist movements in Africa, did not make its presence felt in Cameroon in the early years of the Plan since the economy was expanding during that period. It was not until the 1955 downturn of the economy and the termination of the major construction projects that this group intensified and began to coordinate its opposition to French economic domination.

To meet the demands of the Plan, the number of Europeans grew consistently in Cameroon during the period 1946–1956. But much of the business activity thus initiated was of a marginal nature as it largely depended on the major construction projects. At the same time, however, the double college electoral system guaranteed that the European community had a highly disproportionate representation in the territorial and metropolitan assemblies. The *colons*, together with their metropolitan allies, were able to exert pressure on successive governments and administrations to restrict the level of economic and social advancement of the territory. They also contributed to the elimination of the UPC which they viewed as the greatest threat to their interests. After the party became illegal in July 1955 it was forced into an armed struggle which began in December 1956. This conflict lasted several years and cost the lives of thousands of people.

By the mid-1950s, the decline of large-scale investments and the resulting slowdown in economic activity aggravated discontent among almost all major groups in Cameroonian society. These groups included the "bureaucratic bourgeoisie" and the trade and rural *bourgeoisie* who were excluded from political and social rule by Europeans, the planters who sought increased export quotas, the traders prevented from obtaining licenses for import-export business, the aspiring urban entrepreneurs who were refused a mortgage by the banks, the proletariat and sub-proletariat who had great difficulties finding work. All these groups joined together to reach one overriding conclusion: the political and economic structures of colonialism had become shackles to their expansion. They supported the demand for independence which Cameroon achieved on January 1, 1960, under a regime which was favorable to maintaining close financial, economic, military and political ties with France.[1]

In most of the former French territories of Black Africa, independence temporarily increased hardship rather than reducing it. Cameroon, however, was an exception. During the five years following Independence, Cameroon had a surplus balance of trade, in spite of an increase in financial expenditures. The trade balance regained its former surplus levels and the country accounted for 40 percent of all exports from Equatorial Africa. Statistics cited by President Ahidjo in a speech delivered at the Federal Assembly on April 21, 1965 show that: from 1959 to 1964, Cameroon's exports and imports increased by 25 percent and 27 percent respectively; the federal gross domestic product rose from 54 to 65 billion CFA Francs, a 20 percent increase in spite of a fall in world prices; the industrial production increased from 11 to nearly 20 billion CFA Francs, a 73 percent increase; 35 new enterprises were created, an investment of 2 billion CFA Francs; finally total revenues increased from 12 to 30 billion CFA Francs despite the reduction of 8 billion in French subsidies.[2]

After independence France continued to grant Cameroon financial aid (41 billion CFA Francs between 1959 and 1970 according to *Le Monde Diplomatique* of September 1971) and to invest. Many factors encouraged French investment in post-independent Cameroon. First, independence was not followed by nationalization. Secondly, Cameroon has been enjoying relative peace and stability since independence. Thirdly, the Cooperation Agreements which Cameroon and the other French territories in Black Africa were forced to sign with France have enabled the French to protect their investors and businessmen operating in the territory. Fourthly, because of Cameroon's membership in the franc zone, the movement of capital into and out of the country is relatively easy and there are only minimal restrictions on the export of profits. Finally, Cameroon's policies on foreign investment have been designed to encourage and attract funds to the country. Limits on foreign ownership are few, and partnerships between Cameroonians and foreign investors are not required; the Government also provides various benefits, such as tariff and tax exemptions, to entice foreign investors. As a result French investments have remained significant.[3]

Today, France is Cameroon's major commercial, military, political and cultural partner. The frequency of top-level contact between the two countries has led to a pragmatic relationship based on a history of long-standing mutual interests. However, Cameroon's attempts to lessen its economic dependence on France have led to a reduction of France's role as a purchaser of exports and source of imports. Also, French predominance in the field of investment has been weakening. France's percentage of the total capital held by foreigners in the Cameroonian economy has dropped from 77.4 percent in 1973 to 60.8 percent in 1982. Many Cameroonians argued that government policies have not done enough to protect domestic investors. Since the late 1980s, the Cameroonian government has paid serious attention to redressing this complaint. Meanwhile the colonial legacy continues to affect Cameroon.

NOTES

1. For a more in-depth discussion of the period after 1956 read LeVine (V.T.).; Bayart (J.F.); and Gardinier (D. E.).
2. *Bulletin de l'Afrique Noire*, 369 (April 28, 1965): 7464, and *Perspectives Africaines*, 166 (February 3, 1965): 7.
3. In 1983, for example, French sources represented more than 50 percent of investment in public works, general commerce, and the metal and electric industries. French funds also contributed more than 30 percent of the investment in the fishing, chemical, and food industries (M. Delancy, *Cameroon. Dependence and Independence*, Darmouth: Westview Press, 1989, p. 111).

Appendix
Colonial Companies in French Cameroon by 1956

Financial Institutions

Banque de l'Afrique Occidentale (BAO)
Banque Commerciale Africaine (BCA)
Banque Nationale pour le Commerce et l'Industrie (BNCI)
Caisse Centrale de la France d'Outre Mer (CCFOM)
Crédit de l'AEF
Crédit du Cameroun (CREDICAM)
Crédit Foncier de l'Ouest Africain (CFOA)
Crédit Lyonnais
Société d'Etudes de Gestion de l'Afrique Noire (SEGEDAN)
Société Générale
Société Immobilière et Financière Africaine
Société Financière pour le Développement du Cameroun

Agricultural and Commercial Companies

Les Assureurs-conseils Camerounais (insurance; branch of Mutuelles du Mans)
L'Auxiliaire colonial (farming; pastoralism)
Bois Africain Tropicaux (forestry; export of lumber)
Les Bois du Cameroun (forestry; sawmill)
Les Bois ouvrés de Yaoundé (BOY—forestry; production of lumber goods)
Bongola Lokundji Nyong (BLN—import-export of rubber)
Société Française Bunge (SFB—import-export of agricultural raw materials)
Les Cafés du Cameroun (farming)
La Commerciale de l'Afrique française (COAF—import-export; car sale)
Compagnie Africaine Franco-Anglaise (CAFA—general import-export)
Compagnie Agricole et Forestière du Cameroun (forestry; export of agricultural raw materials)
Compagnie des Bananes (farming; import-export of agricultural goods)
Compagnie Commerciale Cameroun (general import-export)
Compagnie Foncière et Industrielle Africaine (CFIA—real estate)
Compagnie Sangha-Oubangui (CFSO - forestry; farming, mining, import-export)
Compagnie Française de l'Afrique Occidentale (CFAO—general import-export)
Compagnie Commerciale Hollando-Africaine (CCHA—forestry)

Compagnie Française de Dépôts Pétroliers au Cameroun (CFDPC—development and running of hydrocarbons depots)
Compagnie générale de Commerce extérieur (CGCE Cameroun—general import-export)
Compagnie de l'Industrie Textile Cotonnière (CITEC; export of agricultural and textile products)
Compagnie Ouest-Cameroun (COC—exploitation and export of coffee)
Compagnie Pastorale Africaine (PASTORALE—pastoralism)
Compagnie Soudanaise (CS—import-export)
Comptoirs et Plantations du Cameroun (CPC—agricultural and industrial products)
Comptoirs Réunis du Cameroun (CRC—import-export)
C.N. Rossides et Compagnie (Import-export; farming)
Desrotour et chaffaujon (import-export)
Etablissements Emile Nassif et fils (general import-export)
Etablissements R. Guiol (import of wine, liquor, and other goods)
Francis et Baur Ltd (import-export; transportation; plantation)
Franco-coloniale d'assurance (FCA—insurance)
Groupement Français d'Assurance (GFA—insurance)
Imprimerie Commerciale du Cameroun (ICC—printing)
John Holt Compagny (Liverpool) Ltd (insurance)
King (Richard et W.Ltd King (import-export of cars; GMG Chevrolet and Land-Rover dealer)
Lehoux et Compagnie (import-export of cocoa)
Madubo (general import-export)
Mavromatis, Frères (general import-export)
Panafric (general import)
Paterson Zochonis et Co Ltd (PZ—general import-export)
Plantations de Nyombe-Penja (banana, coffee, and palm plantations)
Plantations Réunies de l'Ouest Africain (farming; export of agricultural raw materials)
Plantations des Terres rouges (forestry)
Proca Afrique (general import-export)
Société Africaine Forestière et Agricole (SAFA—forestry; sawmill; production of agricultural raw materials)
Société Africaine de Représentations Industrielles et Commerciales (SAFRIC Cameroun—import of commercial and industrial goods)
Société Africaine de Représentations Industrielles et Automobiles (SARIA—car sale; branch of Hotchkiss and "salev")
Société des Bois Tropicaux (SBT—forestry)
Société Bordelaise Africaine (services)
Société Camerounaise d'Exportations (SOCAMEX—export)
Société Commerciale Camerounaise (SOCOCAM—import-export)
Société Commerciale Industrielle et Agricole du Cameroun (CIAC; import-export of agricultural products)
Société Commerciale Industrielle et Agricole du Haut-Ogoué (import-export)
Société Commerciale de l'Ouest Africain (SCOA—financial, industrial, and commercial services)
Société d'Exploitation Forestière Africaine (SEFA—forestry; sawmill)
Société d'Exploitation Forestière et Industrielle du Cameroun (SEFIC—forestry; sawmill; transit equipment)
Société Générale de Distribution au Cameroun (SODICAM—import-export, transit)
Société d'Importation et d'Exportation du Matériel Industriel (SIEMI—production and import-export of industrial equipment)

Société Industrielle des Cacao (SIC—exploitation of cocoa)
Société Industrielle et Commerciale Protom (general import-export)
Société Inter-colonies (SINC—import-export)
Société Métallurgique et Industrielle Africaine (SOMETINA—import-export of metallurgical and industrial equipment)
Société Nationale du Cameroun (SNC—forestry; sawmill; export of lumber)
Société des Plantations de Djongo-Penja (SPDP; farming; banana and coffee plantations)
Société des Plantations de Foumban (SPF—plantation)
Société Tropicale de Droguerie (STD—pharmacy and drugs wholesale)
Société des Vins du Cameroun (SOVINCA—import-export of wine)
Tissus K. M. (production and export of textile)
"Tract-Afric" (Import of motorized and electrical equipment)
Triandafillidis et Jacovidis (Import of textile and other goods)
Union Traiding Cameroun (UTC—general import-export)
Valor (import and sale of steel goods)
F. Vanier (arm and ammunition dealer)
Warner (import-export; production of sodas)

Industrial Companies (Public Works, Transportation, Mining)

Air Liquide (manufacturing of chemicals and public work accessories)
Alucam (production of aluminum)
Baudon (public works; construction)
Bourdin et Chaussé (public work; construction; sanitation)
Brasserie du Cameroun (brewery)
Cameroun Automobile (sale of auto parts)
Camerounaise de produits chimiques (CPC—manufacturing of bleach)
Chantiers et Ateliers de Douala (CADO—mechanics; maintainance; naval repair; welding)
Compagnie Coloniale de Distribution d'Energie Electrique (CCDEE—electrical works, lighting, heating, engineering)
Compagnie Congolaise pour l'Industrie; (CCI—smelting works, mechanical workshops, electrical and metallurgical works)
Compagnie d'Entreprise Electrique (ENTRELEC—production of electrical industrial equipment; transportation of electricity)
Compagnie Equatoriale des Mines (CEM—mining)
Compagnie d'Exploitation Automobile du Cameroun (CEAC—Renault dealer; car and appliance sale and services, transportation)
Compagnie Générale du Golfe de Guinée (CGG—transportation; forestry; maintainance)
Compagnie Minière du Cameroun (CMC—mining)
Compagnie Minière de l'Oubangui Oriental (CMOO—gold and diamond mining)
Construction et Métaux du Cameroun (COMECA—production of hardware and steel goods)
C.T.C (Sawmill)
Davum Cameroun (production, maintainance, and sale of various industrial goods and equipment)
Descours et Cabaud (production of public works equipment and chemical, métallurgical, and agricultural goods)
Energie Electrique du Cameroun (ENELCAM—production, transportation, and distribution of electricity)

Les Etains du Cameroun (mining)
Hersent (public works)
J. Heudebert et Compagnie (installation and maintenance of mechanical and electrical equipment)
Mory et Compagnie (international transit and transportation)
Société Meunier-Cameroun (public works, construction, electrification)
Société Africaine de Transit d'Affrètement (SATA—transit)
Société Anonyme des Entreprises A. Monod (public works; construction)
Société Anonyme des anciens établissements Joseph Paris (construction)
Entreprises Razel Frères (public works)
Régie Générale des Chemins de fer et des Travaux Publics (public works)
Société Africaine de béton manufacturé (SABM—manufacturing of concrete)
Société Africaine d'Emballages Métalliques (SADEM—metallic packing)
Société Africaine de Travaux et d'Equipements Industriels (SATEI—public works; construction)
Société d'Application du Ciment Armé pour la France d'Outre Mer (SACAFOM—public and concrete works; transportation of electricity)
Société d'Application Electrique au Cameroun (SAEC—transportation and installation of electricity)
Société Camerounaise d'Entreprise de Transport et de Transit (transportation and transit)
Société Camerounaise de Production Chimique (CPC—production of chemicals)
Société Camerounaise de Travaux Publics (SCTP—public and private works)
Société Commerciale des Ports de l'Afrique Occidentale (SOCOPAO—commerce; transit; transportation)
Société de Construction des Batignolles (SCB—public works; construction; sanitation)
Société "Eau et Assainissement" (exploitation and distribution of water)
Société d'Entreprises Chimiques et Routières au Cameroun (SECRAC—public works; production of public work equipment)
Société Française d'Entreprise de Dragage et de Travaux Publics (SFEDTP—public works; metallurgical construction)
Société Immobilière Cameroun-Oubangui (SICO—construction; real estate)
Société Navale Delmas-Vieljeux (SNDV—transit and transportation)
Société Ouest Africaine d'Entreprise Maritime (transportation; transit; barge and truck repair)
Société des Participations Minières en Afrique Centrale (PARMINAC—gold and diamond mining)
Société de Recherche et d'Exploitation des Pétroles du Cameroun (SEREPCA—hydrocarbon prospection and exploitation)
Société des Etablissements Brossette au Cameroun (sale of industrial and public works equipment)
Société des Transports Oubangui-Chari (STOC—transportation)
Le Soliditit Français (public works)
Union Maritime et commerciale (UMARCO—maritime transportation and transit)

Bibliography

This work is based on sources collected in Cameroon, France, and the United States, as well as interviews with Cameroonians who had particular information on some of the issues analyzed in this book because of their research activities and interest, or their personal contacts.

The unpublished documents that were used for this work include doctoral dissertations, and diploma theses written by French colonial administrators during their training at the former *Ecole Nationale de la France d'Outre Mer* (ENFOM—National School of Overseas France). These sources, which can be found at the *Archives Nationales, section d'Outre Mer* (National Archives, Overseas section) in Aix-en-Provence, France, were useful for the analysis of the social and economic development of Cameroon. The importance of these documents comes from the fact that they are based on the local archives of various regions of Cameroon and on research conducted there. However, cross-checking and comparing with other sources were necessary when using these unpublished theses because their quality and reliability vary greatly.

The documents of the United Nations Organization are an important source for research on the history of Cameroon. The United Nations publications used in this study include: French Government annual reports on Cameroon, the sessions of the Trusteeship Council and the General Assembly, the reports of the United Nations missions to Cameroon, and many petitions sent to the United Nations by Cameroonians.

Research to write this book was conducted in the following libraries: *Bibliothèque de Documentation Internationale Contemporaine* (BDIC—Library of Contemporary International Documentation) of the University Paris X-Nanterre and *Documentation Française* (French Documentation) in Paris, which have many books, articles, and studies on Cameroon; *Bibliothèque Nationale* (National Library) in Paris and particularly its Annex (*Bibliothèque Nationale Annexe*) in Versailles where an important collection of Cameroonian newspapers and complete series of colonial periodicals are kept; *Institut National de la Statistique et des Etudes Economiques* (INSEE—National Institute of Statistic and Economic Studies) in Paris, which contains some studies and statistics on Cameroon; and the *Dag Hammarskjold Library* of the United Nations in New York which has many documents of the Trusteeship Council and the General Assembly of the United Nations.

Much of this work is based on archives found in Cameroon, France, and the United Nations. In addition to letters and administrative documents, the *Archives Nationales, section d'Outre Mer* (ANSOM—National Archives, Overseas section) in Aix-en-Provence have a precious collection of books and articles on Cameroon and the other countries that were under French rule. The *Archives Nationales* (National Archives) of Cameroon in Yaoundé are rich in administrative reports, periodicals, and pamphlets. The archives of the United Nations not only have reports and studies on Cameroon but also many letters and petitions from Cameroonians. Finally, two files with useful information were found in the archives of *Institut Charles de Gaulle* (Charles de Gaulle Institute) in Paris.

ARCHIVES

Archives Nationales, section d'outre mer (ANSOM—National Archives, Overseas section), Aix-en-provence

Affaires Economiques files

84 and 85. "Mission Cavet au Cameroun," 1950–1951 (Report on private investment in Cameroon).
101. "Procès-verbal de la Commission de l'économie impériale (1944)."
277. "Cameroun. Mission Mazodier, 1953–1954."
512. *Institut d'Emission d'AEF-Cameroun* monthly reports (1955–1958).
521. CCFOM monthly reports (1946–1957).
538. "Cameroun. Plan de développement économique et social, rapport d'exécution (30 décembre- 30 juin 1951)."
539, 542–560. FIDES second-year plan, 1953–1957.
622–624. *Institut d'Emission d'AEF-Cameroun* various documents (1950–1959).
631. Documents on the economic and monetary development of French West Africa and Cameroon (1950–1959).

FIDES files

7. Various Statistical datas.
29. Reports on the budgetary situation of Cameroon (until 1958).
30. CCFOM monthly reports (1947–1956).
32. "Mission Cavet au Cameroun," 1950–1951 (report on private investment in Cameroon).
44, 54, and 127. Documents on loans granted to various private companies in Cameroon.
50. CCFOM documents (1951–1958).
50 to 122. Documents on public and semi-public companies (IHRO, BMFOM, ORSTOM,

IGN, IFRFOM, IRCT, CGOT, CFDT, ALUCAM, ENELCAM, BRP, BCEEOM, BDPA, BRGM).

73 and 201. Documents on the FIDES second four-year plan (1953–1957).

207. "Plan de modernisation et d'équipement. Premier rapport de la Commission de modernization des territoires d'outre-mer, janvier 1948. Etat des opérations, 1949. Deuxième plan: rapport général des commissions de production agricole et équipement rural 1953. Rapport général des commissions d'étude et de coordination des plans de modernisation et d'équipement des territoires d'outre mer, 1954" (Reports on the implementation and execution of the FIDES program in overseas territories).

351–358. Reports on the FIDES first and second Four-Year plans, economic development, and the financial situation in Cameroon (1946–1957).

407–415. Documents on FIDES investment, overseas section (1952–1959).

416–417. Reports on the state of CCFOM (1947–1952).

506–511. Various reports and datas on loans granted to Camerron by FIDES (1952–1959).

524. The development of the FIDES program in Cameroun (1947–1956).

902. Various information on Cameroon's economy (1949–1953).

Archives Nationales du Cameroun (Cameroon National Archives), Yaoundé

1AC 23, 153, 220, 254, 501, 503, 505, 506, 507(9), 510, 510(1), 511, 1305, 7450, 8104, 8311, 8562. Various reports on the financial situation of Cameroon, FIDES, the budget of Cameroon, and *Crédit du Cameroun* - CREDICAM (1949–1963).

2AC 6853, 6978, 7661, 9403, 9404, 9651. Documents on various private and semi-public companies.

NF 746. "Conférence Financière des Territoires d'Afrique (11 février 1952)."

NF 245/12 et 585/11. Financial reports presented at the Assembly of Cameroon in 1951 and 1952.

NF 74/8, 137, 249/11, 463/10, 463/14, 262/12, 426/12, 74/16, 249/20. Letters on financial issues, 1950-1953.

Institut Charles de Gaulle Archives, Paris

60–61. Correspondences of de Gaulle's party, *Rassemblement Pour la France*. Various administrative reports. Roland Pré file. Documents on the economic and political situation in Cameroon.

United Nations Archives, New York

RAG 2/130 files

2, 3, 130/04(1). Cameroon under French administration (1952–1955).

7, 130/3/03. Annual reports, Cameroon.

9–12, 130/4/01(1), 130/5/01, 130/5/02; 19–36, 130/5/02; 75–79, 130/5/03. Various reports by the French colonial administration, unions, and political organizations. Letters, petitions, and memorandums sent by the people, political organizations, unions, traditional associations, and various organizations of Cameroon to the United Nations (1948–1957).

DAG 5/2.3 files

1. Documents on Cameroon under French rule (1953–1958).
2. Documents on public financing in Cameroon (1955).

DAG 5/2.4 files

3 and 4. Various petitions (1946–1955).

Documents of the United Nations General Assembly

"Accords de Tutelle pour le territoire du Cameroun sous administration française tel qu'il a été approuve par l'Assemblée Générale le 13 décembre 1946."

"Mission de visite de l'ONU dans les Territoires sous tutelle d'Afrique occidentale, 1952). Rapport sur le Cameroun sous administration française et documents y afférents" (Conseil de Tutelle, documents officiels, treizième session, 28 janvier–25 mars 1954, supplément 5, New York: 1954).

"Mission de visite des Nations-Unies dans les Territoires sous tutelle du Cameroun sous l'administration britannique et du Cameroun sous administration française (1955). Rapport sur le Cameroun sous administration française et documents y afférents" (Documents officiels, dix septième session, 7 février - 6 avril 1956, supplément 4, New York: 1956).

"Mission de visite des Nations Unies dans les Territoires sous tutelle de l'Afrique occidentale (1958). Rapport sur le Cameroun sous administration française et documents y afférents" (Conseil de Tutelle, documents officiels, vingt troisième session, 30 janvier–20 mars 1959, supplément 3, New York: 1959).

"Rapport Annuel du Gouvernement Français à l'Assemblée Générale des Nations Unies sur l'Administration du Cameroun placé sous la Tutelle de la France" (Paris: Imprimerie Ch. Lazauzelle, 1947–1958).

"Rapport de la Mission de visite des Nations Unies dans les Territoires sous tutelle d'Afrique occidentale et documentation connexe, supplément 2" (Documents officiels de la septième session du Conseil de Tutelle, 1er juin–21 juillet 1950, Paris: 1951).

"Rapport spécial du Conseil de Tutelle sur les unions administratives concernant les Territoires sous tutelle et sur le statut du Cameroun et du Togo sous administration française tel qu'il résulte de l'appartenance de ces territoires à l'Union française" (New York: 1952).

STATISTICAL DOCUMENTS

"Annuaire Noria. Guide économique AOF-Togo-Cameroun-AEF" (Paris: Larose, 1952–1956).

"Annuaire Statistique de l'AEF" (1950 on).

"Annuaire Statistique du Cameroun" (Paris Imprimerie nationale).

"Annuaire Statistique de l'Union Française" (1939 on).

"Annuaire Statistique de la zone franc" (Paris: Imprimerie nationale, 1949–1955).

"Bulletin Mensuel de Statistique" (Yaoundé: R.F. Cameroun).

"Bulletin Mensuel de Statistique d'Outre Mer" (Paris: Service des statistiques du Ministère de la France d'Outre Mer, 1947 on).

"Cameroun Français. Budget des recettes et des dépenses" (Yaoundé: Imprimerie du gouvernement, 1946 on).

"Commerce extérieure du Cameroun oriental, 1946–1966" (Yaoundé: Présidence de la République).
"Commerce extérieur des Etats d'Afrique et de Madagascar, de 1949 à 1960" (INSEE).
"Documents Statistiques du Ministère de la France d'Outre Mer" (Paris: Service des statistiques du Ministère de la France d'outre mer, 1949 on).
"Les investissements dans les territoires d'outre mer en Afrique au sud du Sahara" (Paris: OECE, 1951).
"Les investissements publics nationaux et extérieurs dans les pays francophones d'Afrique tropicale, 1946–1960," Vol.1 and 2 (Paris: IEDES, 1964).
"Institut d'Emission de l'AEF et du Cameroun. Rapport d'activité" (1955–1957).
"Rapports annuels du Comité monétaire de la zone franc" (Paris: Imprimerie nationale, 1954 on).

PERIODICALS

Banque Centrale des Etats de l'Afrique Equatoriale et du Cameroun (formerly known as Institut d'Emission de l'Afrique Equatoriale Française et du Cameroun).
Bulletin d'Information et de Documentation.
Le Cameroun Libre.
Chroniques d'Outre Mer.
Climats.
Encyclopédie Mensuelle d'Outre Mer.
Journal des Débats de l'Assemblée Territoriale du Cameroun.
Journal Officiel du Cameroun.
Journal Officiel de la République Française.
Marchés Tropicaux et Méditerranéens (formerly known as Marchés Coloniaux du Monde).
Notes et Etudes Documentaires
La Nouvelle Revue Française d'Outre Mer (formerly known as Bulletin de la France d'Outre Mer).

GENERAL BIBLIOGRAPHY

Assale, C. et al. 1950. "Définition d'une politique économique, sociale et monétaire d'ensemble des pays de l'Union française," *Journal Officiel de la République Française* (February 16).
Barbé, R. 1957. "Quelques données économiques sur la crise du système colonial français," *Economie et Politique* (July): 14–36.
Bloch-Lainé, F. 1956. *La zone franc*. Paris: P.U.F.
Bonnefous, E. 1964. *Les milliards qui s'envolent. L'aide française aux pays sous développés*. Paris: Fayard.
Bourcier de Carbon, L. 1952. "L'investissement et les problèmes de développement économiques dans les territoires africains," *Les Cahiers économiques* (June–July).
———. 1952. "Le crédit et l'organisation bancaire," *Marchés Coloniaux* (May 17).
———. 1951. "L'investissement dans les territoires dépendants," Paris: ISEA, serie A, *Plan monétaires internationaux* 8 and 9.
Bourdillon (ed.), 1991. *Les travaux publics français en Afrique subsaharienne et Madagascar 1945–85*. Paris: l'Harmattan.
1952. "Cinq ans d'exécution du Plan de modernisation et d'équipement de l'Union Française. réalisations 1947–1951 et programme 1952." Paris: Commissariat Général au Plan de

modernisation et d'équipement.
1948. "Commissariat Général du Plan de Modernisation et d'Equipement. Premier Rapport de la Commission de Modernisation des TOM" (January).
1955. "Conférence (XXXIXe et XXXe) des chambres de commerce de la Méditerranée et de l'Afrique française. Situation économique du Cameroun." Marseille.
1945. *La Conférence Africaine Française. Brazzaville. 30 janvier 1944–8 février 1944.* Paris: Ministère des Colonies.
Coquery-Vidrovitch, C. 1973. "Commerce, investissement et profits dans l'outre mer français, 1900–1960," RCP 36, Laboratoire Connaissance du Tiers monde. Paris VII and CNRS.
1956. "Dix années d'investissement public dans les territoires d'outre mer," *l'Economie* 539 (May 10).
DeLancy, M. and DeLancy, M.D., 2000. *Historical Dictionary of the Republic of Cameroon.* Lanham : The Scarecrow Press, Inc.
Dumaine, A. 1955. "La signification réelle du second plan d'équipement et de modernisation des territoires d'outre mer," *Présence Africaine* (April–July).
Durand, H. 1957. *Essai sur la conjoncture de l'Afrique noire.* Paris: Dalloz.
1949–57. "Fonds de Développement Economique et Social. Rapports de la Commission des Investissements."
1956–57. "Le fonds d'investissement pour le développement économique et social des territoires d'outre mer," *Présence Africaine* (December–January).
Hoffher, R. 1958. *Coopération économique franco-africaine.* Paris: Sirey.
Imbert, J. 1982. *Le Cameroun.* Paris : Presses Universitaires de France.
Jacobson, A. 1957. "Le Problème des investissements dans la France d'outre mer," *Revue Economique Française* 4 (November): 14–22.
Jean-François, A. 1930. *La France et la mise en valeur de ses colonies.* Paris: Imprimerie des Presses Modernes.
Jeanneney, J. 1964. *La politique de coopération avec les pays en voie de développement.* Paris: La Documentation Française.
———. 1959. *Forces et faiblesses de l'économie française.* Paris: A. Colin.
Jeanneny, J. and Barbier Jeanneny, E. 1985. *Les économies occidentales du XXe siècle à nos jours.* Paris: FNSP.
Juliette, R. 1954. "La situation financière des pays d'outre mer et le Trésor public," *Economie Appliquée* 4 (October–December): 377–402.
Du Jonchay, I. 1953. *L'Industrialisation de l'Afrique.* Paris: Payot.
Lattre, A. de. 1979. *Histoire de la politique économique française de 1945 à 1977.* Paris: IEP.
———. 1959. *Les finances extérieures de la France.* Paris: P.U.F.
Lattre, J.M. de. 1954. *La mise en valeur de l'ensemble eurafricain français et le participation des capitaux étrangers, sociétés à participation étrangère, compagnies à charte.* Paris: LGDJ.
Lawrence, A. 1956. "Les investissements dans les territoires d'outre mer," *JORF, Conseil Economique, avis et rapports* (March 7): 105–135.
Lecaillon, J. 1953. "La place de l'Union française dans l'équilibre financier métropolitain," *Revue de Science et de Législation financière* (April–June).
Leduc, G. 1957. "La politique des investissements dans l'outre mer," Revue des Sciences Financières 1 (January-March): 94–115.
———. 1955. *Le développement économique de l'Afrique noire.* Paris: Cujas.
———. 1952. "La politique fiscale d'encouragement aux investissements des pays d'outre mer," *Revue des Sciences et de Législation Financière* (October–December).
———. 1951. "Aspects financiers, fiscaux, et budgétaires du développement des pays sous

développés," *Travaux de l'Institut International des finances publiques*. London.
Ligot, M. 1964. *Les accords de coopération entre la France et les Etat africains et malgache d'expression française*. Paris: La Documentation Française.
Manue, G. 1962. "De l'ère coloniale à la coopération," *Revue des deux mondes* (Jan 15): 13–18.
Marseille, J. 1984. *Empire colonial et capitalisme français. Histoire d'un divorce*. Paris: Albin Michel.
———. 1982. "L'industrialisation des colonies: affaiblissement ou renforcement de la puissance française?" *Revue Française d'Histoire d'Outre mer* 254.
Moreux, R. 1951. *Principes nouveaux d'économie coloniale*. Paris.
Moussa, P. 1960. *L'économie de la zone franc*. Paris: P.U.F.
———. 1957. *Les chances économiques de la communauté franco-africaine*. Paris: A. Colin.
Ndongo, S. 1972. *La coopération franco-africaine*. Paris: Maspero.
Ngango, G. 1973. *Les investissements d'origine extérieure en Afrique noire francophone: statut et incidences sur le développement*. Paris: Présence Africaine.
Ossende Afana. 1966. *L'économie de l'Ouest africain*. Paris: Maspero.
Picquemal. 1957. "Les exportations de capitaux français dans les colonies," *Economie et Politique* (August–September): 66–75.
———. 1955. "Les mouvements des capitaux français vers l'outre mer," *Revue des Sciences et de Législation Financière* (October–December).
Postel-Vinay, A. 1951. "Aspects financiers et budgétaires du développement économique de l'Union française," in "Les aspects financiers, fiscaux et budgétaires du développement des pays sous développés. Rapport des travaux de la 7e session de l'Institut International des Finances Publiques, Londres" (September): 170–193.
1949. "Rapport du Commissariat Général sur le plan de modernisation et d'équipement de l'Union française, réalisation 1947–1949 et objectifs 1950–1952." Paris: Présidence du Conseil.
Saint Marc, M. 1964. *Zone franc et décolonisation*. Paris: Société d'édition d'enseignement supérieur.
Servoise, R. 1953. "Problèmes généraux des investissements dans les pays sous développés," *Cahiers économiques* (February).
———. 1949. "Les investissements publics en Afrique noire", *L'Economie* (March 16).
Suret-Canale, J. 1977. *Afrique noire occidentale et centrale, T3, De la décolonisation aux indépendances, 1945–1960, vol.1, Crise du système colonial et capitalisme monopoliste d'Etat*. Paris: Editions Sociales.
1954. "Les trusts français aux colonies," *Economie et Politique* 5–6: 99–124.

BIBLIOGRAPHY ON CAMEROON

Alexandre, P. and BINET, J. 1958. *Le groupe dit Pahouin (Fang-Boulou-Beti)*. Paris: P.U.F.
Antoine, P. 1954. "Les Sociétés Africaines de Prévoyance au Cameroun," FDSE, 1954.
Atangana, M. 2001. "Mythes et réalités de l'investissement privé en Afrique noire française: le cas du Cameroun dans les années 1940 et 1950," *Canadian Journal of African Studies* 35, no. 1: 1–31.
———. 1998. *Capitalisme et nationalisme au Cameroun au lendemain de la seconde guerre mondiale, 1946–1956*. Paris : Les Publications de la Sorbonne.
———. 1997. "French Capitalism and Nationalism in Cameroon," *African Studies Review* 40, no. 1 (April): 83–111.

———. 1993. "Les relations financières entre le Cameroun et la France et l'image de la France au Cameroun, 1946–1956," *Matériaux* 32–33 (July–December): 47–52.

Aubery, M.R. 1957. "La situation économique du Cameroun en 1956," *Etudes d'outre mer* 9 (November): 335–344.

Awana, C. 1958. "Evolution de la chefferie traditionnelle en pays beti (sud Cameroun)," ENFOM 122.

Binet, J. 1961. "Les cadres au Cameroun," *Civilisations* 11, no. 1: 21–36.

———. "Les budgets familiaux du sud Cameroun, 1954–1956," IRCAM.

———. 1956. "Budgets familiaux des planteurs de cacao au Cameroun," Collection L'Homme d'outre mer 3, ORSTOM.

———. 1955. "Cameroun: structures politiques coutumières," *Encyclopédie Mensuelle d'outre mer* 5, no. 63 (November).

———. 1954. "Cacao au Cameroun," *Encyclopédie Mensuelle d'outre mer* 4, no. 52 (December): 340–344.

Bouchart, P. 1956. "Le FIDES au Cameroun," *Civilisation* 6, no. 3: 393–409.

"Cameroun 1952," *Marchés Coloniaux* 340 (May 17): 1237–1418.

"Cameroun français. Budget des recettes et des dépenses (1949–1955)." Yaoundé: Imprimerie du gouvernement.

"Cameroun 1959," *Marchés Tropicaux et Méditerranéens* 732 (November 21): 2527–2633.

"Cameroun 1952," *Marchés Coloniaux* 340 (May 17): 1237–1418.

Chaffard, G. 1959. "Le Cameroun à la veille de l'indépendance," *Europe-France outre mer* 355 (June): 25–51).

Chauleur, P. 1959. "Le Cameroun à la veille de l'indépendance," *Etudes* 11 (November): 202–214.

———. 1955. "La transformation du Cameroun," *Encyclopédie Mensuelle d'outre mer* 4, fasc. 54 (February): 71–76.

———. 1954. "L'industrialisation du Cameroun et ses perspectives," *Industries et Travaux d'outre mer* 13 (December): 739–747.

Darge, P. 1959. "Le café au Cameroun," ENFOM 41.

Delancy, M. 1989. *Cameroon. Dependence and Independence*. Darmouth: West view Press.

De Soye, J. and Beaurois, R. 1958. "L'expansion bamiléké," ENFOM 48.

Didier, H. 1954. "Aperçu sur la situation et l'évolution économiques et financières du Cameroun," *La Nouvelle Revue Française d'Outre mer* 4 (April): 150–161.

Dominici, L. 1959. "La banane d'exportation au Cameroun," ENFOM 56.

Edoo, P. 1961. "L'expérience coopérative au Cameroun," FDSE.

Enfoux, P. 1957. "Influence de l'industrialisation actuelle de la Sanaga Maritime sur le développement politique, économique et social de cette région," ENFOM 21.

Eteki-Mboumoua, W. 1959. "De quelques incidents sociaux de l'Alucam," ENFOM 64.

Eyinga, A. 1958–59. "Dix années de FIDES au Cameroun (1947–1957)," ENFOM 66.

Hugon, P. 1968. *Analyse du sous développement en Afrique noire: l'exemple de l'économie du Cameroun*. Paris: P.U.F.

Johnson, W. 1970. *The Cameroon federation: Political Integration in a fragmentary Society*. Princeton: Princeton University Press.

Joseph, R. 1977. *Radical Nationalism in Cameroon. Social Origins of the UPC Rebellion*. Oxford: The Clarendon Press.

Kodock, A. 1967. "Les problèmes du crédit dans le développement économique du Cameroun," FDSE.

Kom, D. 1971. *Le Cameroun: Essai d'analyse économie politique*. Paris: Editions Sociales.

Leduc, G. 1959. "L'évolution des masses et des structures budgétaires du Cameroun et de l'AEF depuis 1929," *Banque Centrale de l'Afrique Equatoriale et du Cameroun* 38 (August–September): 309–320.

Maslin, P. 1952. "Peuplement blanc et mise en valeur de l'ouest Cameroun," ENFOM 20.

Mbongo-Mounoume, T. 1959. "Le paysan beti et la politique du cacao," ENFOM 101.

Mveng, E. 1963. *Histoire du Cameroun.* Paris: Présence Africaine.

Ndogmo, J. 1981. *Le dynamisme bamiléké.* Yaoundé: CEPER.

Ngayewang, P. 1954. "Opinion camerounaise. Important malaise économique," *La Presse du Cameroun* (27 février).

N'nah Nsengue d'Ebolowa. 1975. "Le bilan politique, social et économique de l'administration française au Cameroun, du mandat à la fin de la tutelle (1920–1959)," doctoral dissertation, University of Paris VIII.

"Note sur la situation économique du territoire à la fin de l'Année 1956." Yaoundé: Territoire du Cameroun.

Oyono, D. 1988. "La politique africaine du Cameroun 1960–1985," doctoral dissertation, IEP, Paris.

Pain, F. 1959. "Evolution économique et sociale du Cameroun depuis 1947," FDSE.

Pré, R. 1955. "Presentation of the Cameroon," *Etudes Américaines* 10, Cahier 54: 3–30.

Richard, R. 1957. "Le budget du Cameroun et les investissements du FIDES," thesis, ENA, Paris.

Saulere, P. 1959. "Les planteurs de cacao dans la subdivision de Sangmélima," ENFOM 153.

Schatzberg, M., and Zartman, I. 1986. *The Political Economy of Cameroon.* New York: Praeger.

Um Nyobè, R. 1984. *Le problème national kamerunais*, (edited by J.A. Mbembe). Paris: L'Harmattan.

Index

O

P

R

S

T

U

W

Y

SOCIETY AND POLITICS IN AFRICA

Yakubu Saaka, General Editor

This multidisciplinary series publishes monographs and edited volumes that provide innovative approaches to the study and appreciation of contemporary African society. Although we focus mainly on subjects in the social sciences, we will consider manuscripts in the humanities that treat context as a significant aspect of discourse. Within the social sciences, we are looking for not only analytically outstanding studies but, what is more important, ones that may also have significant implications for the formulation and implementation of public policy in Africa. We are especially interested in works that challenge pre-existing hierarchies and paradigms.

For additional information about this series or for the submission of manuscripts, please contact:

Peter Lang Publishing
Acquisitions Department
29 Broadway, 18th Floor
New York, New York 10006

To order other books in this series, please contact our Customer Service Department:

800-770-LANG (within the U.S.)
(212) 647-7706 (outside the U.S.)
(212) 647-7707 FAX

Or browse online by series at:

www.peterlang.com

www.ingramcontent.com/pod-product-compliance
Ingram Content Group UK Ltd.
Pitfield, Milton Keynes, MK11 3LW, UK
UKHW020209290926
15470UKWH00001B/94

9 781433 104640